Weerz me dad?

A collection of autobiographical
childhood stories of
the 40s and 50s
by Fred Pass

Edited by Hazel Wilkinson

Revised Edition

Copyright Fred Pass 2004

Printed and published by:
ALD Design & Print
279 Sharrow Vale Road
Sheffield S11 8ZF

Telephone 0114 267 9402
E:mail a.lofthouse@btinternet.com

ISBN 1-901587-17-7

First published November 2001
Second Edition March 2004

Cover photograph: Fred Pass aged 5, 1947.

Chapters   Page

This book is dedicated to my mam and dad,

Fred and Gladys Pass

Introduction

This edition of 'Weerz me dad?' is a revision of the book first published in November 2001 which sold almost exclusively in the South Yorkshire region. The revised text includes some additional explanations of the areas in which I grew up, as well as some additional editing to aid continuity.

'Weerz me dad?' is my attempt to relive some moments - a mixture of desperate, happy, miserable, funny times - from my earliest recollections in 1947, at the age of about five years, to the day we left our first home, in 1952. I hope it gives you an idea of the fortitude and grittiness of the people of the time. In saying this, I don't include myself. I was just a little kid who was born into a time of hardship and met the reality of that hardship head on.

My family lived in Martin Street in north central Sheffield. Martin Street, which was cobbled with terraced houses on both sides, ran off Upperthorpe Road, which was at the back of the Sheffield Royal Infirmary, now a supermarket. On the right of the street, the houses were slightly raised by a two-step pavement, where each house had a postage-stamp sized garden. On the left were terraced houses whose continuity was punctured by an entry which went downwards to a yard of back-to-back houses, hence the use of 'court' in their addresses, in our case 19 Court 5.

Although we'd just won a war with Germany, our neighbours and, indeed, the majority of those living in working class areas, still had much to endure. Food rationing for one thing. Desperately poor living conditions, for another. People survived, not in spite of each other, but because of each other. The order of the day was not to keep up with the Joneses, but to survive from one week to the next or in some cases, day to day.

So, this is a sort of a journey of words. I sincerely hope you find something interesting in the journey and the characters you meet along the way.

Fred Pass

Chapter 1

Moving

This is the story of what I can remember of the first ten years of my life. And what ten years they were. So filled with adventure, drama, excitement and emotion that I could never forget them, even if I wanted to, which I don't. Those ten years were spent in Martin Street, in a densely populated area near the centre of Sheffield. Later, during my teenage years, I'd never bring up the subject of Martin Street in conversation. It's not that I was ashamed in any way, but there were two things stopping me. One, I was consciously putting the hard times behind me. Two, I'd yet to develop the maturity to face up to the reality of those experiences.

Martin Street was demolished in 1956. As I can't remember anything before the age of four, knowing where to start a story like this is difficult, so I'll be unconventional and start at the end, on the day we left.

The year was 1952. My mother, my Auntie May and I, were crossing Rutland Bridge to our new home, 19 Boyland Place, Neepsend. We were carrying the last remnants of our belongings from 19 Court 5, Martin Street. My dad had arranged a van for the main items and we had the remaining odds and sods. My mother was carrying a large cardboard box. Auntie May was carrying the goldfish bowl, complete with goldfish, and I was carrying another cardboard box which contained our cat, Topsy. We were leaving our old house in Martin Street which, to be blunt, was a slum.

Nevertheless, it was rich in good people and had provided me with thousands of memories. Some happy, some not.

On the bridge, we passed a policeman. 'Moonlighting, love?' he asked, referring to the age-old fashion, adopted by many of those robbed of their honesty by poverty, of flitting at night in a bid to escape creditors without anyone knowing where they were moving to. The term 'moonlighting' was often a literal one. 'No, we're bloody not,' she snapped back.

Although Boyland Place was less than a mile away from Martin Street, it had numerous advantages. It had two bedrooms, whereas Martin Street had only one. It had a small off-shot kitchen. Martin Street had none. And it had its very own outside toilet. In Martin Street we'd had to share with four other families. The new house was just around the corner from my dad's workplace, 'The Hallamshire Steel and File Rolling Mills', and we'd got it to rent because of my dad's long service. Most of the properties around there belonged to 'the Hallamshire'. Boyland Place was situated smack bang in the middle of the industrialised Neepsend and, environmentally, it was much worse than Martin Street, but the improved living accommodation easily outweighed what were, at the time, little-considered health concerns.

Despite the apparent advantages of the new house, I was a ten year old kid, apprehensive about leaving Martin Street and its store of memories.

Our family consisted of my dad, Fred; mother, Gladys; brother Brian, seven years older than I was, and me. Our 'one up, one down' house in Martin Street, which had been far from ideal for a family of four, had been halfway up on the left-hand side. Martin Street was a hive of back-to-back houses surrounded by streets of smaller dwellings. Our house was in a yard, hence the address, 19 Court 5. To reach our house, you went down a steep entry about eight yards long. The roof of the entry dipped suddenly from about seven foot high at the top of the entry, to about five feet towards the bottom. To bring the abrupt change in height to your notice, a white flash was painted across the dip to remind you to duck your head. Our house faced the entry, across the yard. The yard consisted of seven houses, four on our side, and three on the other.

To the left lived the Murphys, an Irish family. To our right, Mr and Mrs Hill and their son Colin, who was about our Brian's age. Beyond them, in the corner, were the Hoggs - Mr and Mrs, Margaret, who was older than me, and Frank, who was about a year younger than me. The three houses facing had attics. The families in them from the left, facing us, were the Thorpes, the Marshalls and the Aistrops. Mr Thorpe, a widower, had two boys, Les and Stanley, and a daughter, Betty. Mr and Mrs Marshall had three children, Hazel, Margaret and Peter, who was a year younger than me. On the other side of the entry, facing us, were the Aistrops who had six or seven kids. I think Mrs Aistrop must have been married before because their eldest, Audrey, had the surname Fairweather. The names of the other kids have gone from my memory, except Dennis, the eldest of the Aistrop boys, who was my best pal.

The Aistrops were always around when I was a kid. Living across the yard from us, they were an integral part of our lives. Dennis and his brothers and sisters definitely had a harder bringing up than I did. Their dad, Ernest Aistrop, was a small, pleasant bloke who, as well as having all these kids to put up with, didn't always enjoy the best of health. Their mother, Beatrice, was even smaller in stature and always seemed under pressure, which she probably was.

At the time, it seemed to me that she had a baby every other month. Whenever she was in labour the call would go out, 'Beat's ready', and a couple of women, which always included my mother, would dash to help in the birth of the latest Aistrop. The only problem I had with this was that my mother always took me with her. I'd sit downstairs, all the time able to hear the groaning - and sometimes the screaming - of childbirth. Beat could shout like a good 'un, the volume of her voice being best compared to that of the actress Peggy Mount, who was in many British films in the 1950s and, later on, in the early television sitcoms. When she shouted, she really shouted. It left me, to this day, unable to watch someone act out childbirth on television. I know it's not for real, but I still have to leave the room, much to the amusement of my family. And I always tried to be as far away from the action as possible when my own children were being born.

Things were so hard for the Aistrops that when Beat washed the curtains, newspaper would be put up until they were dry enough to go back. And, sometimes, there wouldn't be enough cups to go around so there'd usually be someone or two drinking out of a jam jar. Once, Mrs Aistrop put on a birthday party for Dennis. Despite her poverty, she really tried. I went to that party. All the kids had home-made paper hats on and we all had to make do with a jam jar of tea, slices of bread and dripping, jelly and some tiny buns that one of the neighbours had chipped in with. I remember eating away at a slice of bread and dripping, only to discover a large hair in my mouth. What with that, plus the jam jars full of milky tea with big tea leaves floating around, I immediately started to heave and just wouldn't eat or drink anything else. When this came to Mrs Aistrop's notice, she turned to my mother. 'In't your Fred a funny twat.' After that, she'd often refer to me as 'funny twat' in general conversation.

As every neighbour did in those days, no one knocked on anyone's front door when going in and Mrs Aistrop had a way of entering our house that would startle me every time. She'd hit the knocker on the door and, in one movement, burst in with a bang. 'It's a chuffin' miracle that door's still on its hinges,' my dad would say, without turning a hair. As people did in those days, she'd often come to our house to ask, ''As tha got a drop o' milk?' or 'As tha got a bit of flour?' and so on. She once came to our house asking if she could borrow our frying pan and could she have a bit of fat in it, too. I heard my dad say under his breath, 'Well, Ah've 'eard bleedin' lot now.' Her request today would, I'm sure, seem far-fetched and funny, but it was the reality of life in the forties for many poor families of which the Aistrops were just one. Not that we had anything to brag about. We weren't much better off.

By the look of our house, it must have taken about a week to build. The downstairs room had a cast iron fireplace to the right as you entered, a pot sink alongside and a single gas ring. On the other side of the fireplace were two built-in cupboards, and a long top of about five feet ending with a two-foot bottom cupboard, with a coal cellar in the facing corner. The furniture consisted of a sideboard, a settee, a table and four straight-backed wooden chairs, a lino-covered floor and a pegged rug in front of the fire. It was pretty basic, dictated more by financial limitations than by design.

A wooden stair led up to the bedroom, and at the top of the stair was an alcove that had a curtain hung across the front of it to make an improvised wardrobe. The bedroom had two double beds, about six inches apart - Brian and me in one bed, mam and dad in the other. There was no wallpaper on the walls because rain seeped into them in bad weather, so they were distempered a depressing bluish colour.

For bedding we had woolly jumpers and a couple of old sheets and overcoats, the latter courtesy of my uncle Ern. Many are the times I've laid in bed, twiddling with the brass buttons on those overcoats, remembering some of Uncle Ern's wartime stories. While these conditions were undeniably poor, we were, in some ways, lucky, for there were only four people in our house. Some families of ten, or more, lived in identical conditions.

My first introduction to conflict with authority came about because of the stairs in that house. The wood was so rotten that my brother Brian injured his foot by putting it right through a stair, one morning coming down them. They'd been in a state for ages but, despite several previous pleas by my parents, the landlord had never kept his promise to fix them. So, when this happened, my dad, who was a stocky, gruff-voiced bloke about five feet six tall, took matters into his own hands and demolished the stairs completely with a sledge hammer. He was on 'afternoons' that day and didn't start work until a few hours later, so he waited, with arms folded, for the landlord to arrive for his weekly rent.

We all waited with him with great expectation. If the landlord was good at anything, it was being on time for his rent. When he duly arrived, my dad got hold of him around the neck with one hand, lifted him into the house, pointed at the stairs and said, 'No rent until we get new stairs. And we want new stairs today. **Does tha ger it?**'

The landlord couldn't reply verbally because of the pressure on his neck, but nodded in agreement. The result was success. We had new stairs the very same day.

Chapter 2

Pals

My other main pals, apart from Dennis Aistrop, were Lawrence Jenkinson, who lived on Martin Street itself, at the top of our yard, and little Pete Marshall who lived facing us. Dennis, despite coming from a big family living in harsh conditions, was very bright. When he was about eight years old, people would come from all over our street for him to reckon up their bets. This never failed to impress young and old. Someone would say something like, 'I had three doubles and a treble, Dennis. I've three winners 15 to 8, 6 to 4 and a 13 to 2 and I've had the bet in threepences. What am I owed?' To everyone's amazement, equipped with only a stubby pencil and a scrap of paper, Dennis would work it out in seconds.

He was so bright that, when he was nine, a teacher from our school paid Mrs Aistrop a visit to tell her that he was already capable of passing his eleven-plus, so she should start saving straightaway for his grammar school uniform. The teacher was wasting his breath. Well, just to get by, day by day, was an achievement for Mrs Aistrop. And when you consider the frying pan and bit of fat story, you can see that saving up for a grammar school uniform was the last thing on her list. It was a tragedy, really. Here was a young lad who would often be asked by grown ups to read the evening paper to them, work out gambling odds and all manner of other things, and he was doomed to a life with no prospects of betterment. Dennis must have been a naturally gifted lad. His abilities *must* have been a gift because I never saw any reading material in the Aistrops, apart from the newspaper which was put up when the curtains were being washed.

Lawrence Jenkinson came from an altogether different background. While being by no means privileged, Lawrence was the only child of the family and his mother and dad, who was a part-time copper, both worked full-time. This meant that they were significantly better off than their neighbours. The downside for him was that he spent a lot of time on his own, especially at holiday times. Jenks, as we called him, had ginger hair, glasses and wobbly eyes.

Our main pastime was football, if not on 'the tip' at the top of Martin Street, then in our yard on the street, in fact, anywhere. We had a bit of a reputation in Martin Street and were nicknamed LDV after the Home Guard, otherwise known as the Local Defence Volunteers, who had been renamed by some wartime wag as 'look, duck and vanish' and ultimately by the initials LDV. We'd earned the nickname after several escapades.

Pete Marshall was the first reserve of the gang. He was a little blond kid, much smaller that the rest of us, with freckles. The thing that held Pete back from total and immediate acceptance into the gang was that he always wore hobnailed boots, so, not only could you hear him coming, but when he was running away, you'd also hear exactly where he was going. This was a bit of a draw back when the ability to make a swift, silent escape was a prerequisite of most of our activities, and it robbed him of full membership of the gang for a long time.

One day we were playing football with a tennis ball in Martin Street on the corner of Burlington Street, near the post box, when up trundled the postman in his van. He pulled up and straight away started shouting abuse at us. 'Geroff fuckin' roo-ad, ya little twats.' Somehow I don't think Postman Pat was born out of this character. He then grabbed our tennis ball and kicked it down Burlington Street. We all looked in horror as the ball bounced into the distance. When it reached the bottom, a little kid sprang from nowhere, snatched the ball and disappeared, much to the postman's amusement. He locked up the post box with his jangling keys and bade us farewell with a big smile, saying with undisguised satisfaction, 'That's dun ya.' He didn't know it at the time, but he couldn't have done anything worse.

No ball equalled nothing to do, equalled mischief. Dennis, being the brains of the LDV, checked the post box collection times and reported, 'He'll be back at ten past one tomorrow.' Retribution was then the name of the game. From that moment until ten past one the next day we would, at suitable intervals, do some posting of our own. We let Little Pete join in and he posted a nice slice of bread and treacle. Other mailed items included bread and lard, bread and dripping, dog turds, handfuls of muck, banana skins … in fact anything postable.

The next day, we all perched behind a wall and waited for the postman and, bang on time, he turned up. Our escape plan was already in place in case we were spotted. We'd split up and, after darting through a maze of back yards, meet up at the bottom of Martin Street, leaving old postie looking in the other direction.

He jumped out of his van and looked genuinely disappointed by our absence. He unlocked the post box, whistling his head off and dug his hands deep inside. We waited for the inevitable. 'Oh, fuckin' 'ell!' he bellowed, then looked up, spotted us and began the chase, with all the letters stuck to his hands. No contest. We each disappeared up a different entry, over a couple of walls and, within a minute, we were behind him, chanting 'ner-ner-na-ner-ner', with thumbs on noses and fingers twiddling. He spun round, letters still stuck to his hands, and made another forlorn dash for us, this time slipping on a banana skin and landing face down. At this, Jenks shouted, 'Three cheers for the postman. Hip hip ...' and we all cheered.

Like all pranks we couldn't let it go at that. To us, the score was one all, and we wanted a decider. A few days later, we repeated the exercise. Similar things were posted, only this time we added an inner tube, Dennis posted a pair of their Audrey's knickers, and lumps of wood were cut down and dropped in, followed by Bisto gravy salts, sugar, and salt. Then someone scattered in a box of matches. We each dared the other to light another match and drop it on the top. Inevitably, someone took up the challenge and that person, who remains nameless to this day, did the deed. Within a few seconds, there was a whooshing sound and black smoke and flames began to shoot out of the post box. Without a word being spoken, we all shot off to our respective houses. It was as though we'd transmitted 'abandon ship' by telepathy.

I dashed into our house where my mother was working her way through a pile of ironing. I ran in, sat bolt upright on one of our wooden chairs, never said a word, and looked straight ahead. My mother twigged immediately that something had happened. My body language screamed out 'trouble' with a capital 't'.

'What's up?'
'Eh?'
'What's tha bin doin'?'
'Ah feel sick.'
'Tha'll feel sick if tha't in any trouble.'

The next minute, the fire engine came hurtling up Martin Street with its bells clanging. Even inside the house, it was enough to burst your eardrums as the windows rattled, exposing yet another defect in our jerry-built house.

'What's chuffin' fire engine doin' up 'ere?'
'What fire engine?'
'Tha little chuff. Tha's got somat to do wi' it, ant tha?'

At this, she grabbed me by the hand and took me to the top of our entry to have a look at what was going on. All of Martin Street was out to see the firemen. The post box was now black instead of its customary red. An old bloke remarked casually to my mother, 'It looks like Look, Duck and Vanish 'ave bin at it agee'rn,' observing me closely out of the corner of his eye as he said it. She, unaware of our nickname, answered, 'Ah know what Ah'd do wi 'em. Come on,' she said to me, 'Get in that 'ouse.'

Next day, Lawrence Jenkinson's dad, in his guise as part-time copper, had the job of making enquiries using the 'softly softly' approach. He eventually arrived at our house.

'Nah then, Missis Pass, does your Freddy know owt abaht post box job?'

'No, ee was in all day. Don't thee go accusin' eny o' mah kids wi stuff like that. '

'Nay, Missis Pass, Ah'm not accusing enybody, ony Ah'm tryin' to find owt oo dun it, that's all. Our Lawrence never went owt iver. 'E was bizzy readin'. Missis Aistrop sed their Dennis woz at iz aunties and Missis Marshall sed little Pete woz in bed sick all day.'

'Tha wants to get thi'sen up Mushroom Lane. Thiz sum reight little bleeders up there.'

'OK, Missis Pass, Ah'm sorry fer troubling ya.'

I breathed a sigh of relief.

As soon as he'd gone, I looked up at my mother with a sort of 'thanks, mam' expression on my face. It did no good. She tore into me. 'Ya 'no' you, ya little cow-bag, you'll end up int 'omes if ya don't stop gerrin' inta trouble, an Ah'll tek thee mi'sen.' She really went mad, screaming and shouting and waving her arms about, although she didn't hit me.

What did hit me, was the realisation that each parent had blatantly lied to protect their own, even down to Jenks' dad and he was a copper! Plus the fact that each one knew the other was lying.

Nevertheless, it brought the desired result. We got away with it.

Not long after, I was given a John Bull Printing Set by my Auntie May for my seventh birthday. The set consisted of a complete alphabet of tiny rubber letters, a tin with an inkpad, and a stamper on which you arranged your letters to make words. You then pressed your stamper on the inkpad and then on paper, printing whatever you wanted, as if by magic. The only problem was that every word, and every sentence, had to be done backwards so that it would come out stamped correctly. As I had trouble getting my head around this, it was obviously a job for Dennis.

The first task was to decide what to print. Together we decided on a good phrase. It consisted of two words. The first had four letters and began with 'f' and the second word was 'off'. We tried it out. 'Yes!'

So, armed with John Bull, Dennis, Jenks and I set off down Martin Street with a Beaverbrook 'print and be damned' attitude. We saw a baby in a pram, so we stamped the two words on the soles of its bare feet, its parents in the house, oblivious to our caper.

Next was White's fruit shop. While Dennis was asking Mr White if he had any old apples, I was stamping a box of bananas outside the shop. Mr White was typical of most shop-owners of that era. If you asked him for old apples, he'd go through a box, and if one had started to go rotten, he'd get out his pen-knife, cut away the bad part and chuck you the apple. He'd also give away over-ripe bananas. However, being the little sods we were, Mr White's kindness didn't make him immune to our stunt.

Then, we hit on the perfect subject. On the bottom of

Burlington Street we heard the cry, 'Late night final,' the call of the paper seller who we nicknamed Lionel, sort of 'Lionel with the final'. He was a very friendly bloke who we'd sometimes chat to in moments of boredom.

He greeted us with, 'Hiya lads!' and looked particularly pleased to see us. Obviously, he was close to being ready for a break. Lionel sometimes left his pitch to go for a cup of tea in one of the houses and we'd stand in for him for ten minutes or so. He'd always reward us with a threepenny bit or a tanner, so we got on OK. That day, after standing with him for a bit, he duly said, 'Do us a favour. Ah'm just goin' to 'ave mi cup of tea.' As soon as his back was turned, we got to work like lightening and stamped our two words on all his papers. He came back, gave us a threepenny bit and we were off on our merry way to get a penny ice lolly apiece. Mission accomplished.

A day or so later, Mrs Aistrop came into our house brandishing a banana.

'As tha seen this, Gladys?'
My mother looked at it.

'It'll not mek banana taste eny diff'rent.'

Mrs Aistrop left the house with a 'Don't 'no' what's bleeding goin' on around here lately!' My mother looked at me with glaring eyes.

'Tha'll end up int 'omes, me lad. Ah bet that Dennis 'ad sommat to do wi' this lot, an' all. An' Ah'll tell thee sommat else, thi Auntie May'll not buy thee owt else when Ah tell 'er.'

She'd put two and two together and produced smack on four. She walked over to the drawer, took out the John Bull Printing Set and said, 'A tha lookin'?' Then chucked it on the fire.

Chapter 3

Capers

One day, I noticed that our cat, Topsy, was missing. We all had a think and came to the conclusion that she'd been missing for at least a couple of days. Anyway, that evening my dad opened the cellar door and out dashed Topsy, screeching like mad. Inadvertently, she'd wondered down the cellar and someone, unknowingly, had closed the cellar door. It must have been summer time because, otherwise, it would have been open on a regular basis so that we could get coal for the fire.

On regaining her freedom, old Topsy, after being locked in the dark for so long, went mad to get out of the house. She sprang up the curtains, up the wall and generally scared the life out of us all. Anyway, later that week, the LDV mob, plus Little Pete, were playing football in the street when our ball (which, incidentally, had been nicked from a group similar to ours), accidentally kicked against some miserable sod's door. A woman came to the door shouting, 'If that bleedin' ball 'its our door agee'rn, Ah'm keepin' it!' So, just to test her word, Little Pete obliged, hitting the door with a right foot volley. The woman dashed out, grabbed the ball and snarled, 'That's it, y'ave 'ad it!' No amount of pleading would make her give us our ball back.

Being an inventive sort of bunch, we had to come up with something to get our ball back. I suddenly remembered our Topsy's reaction to being cooped up for a couple of days. After telling the others about it, it was decided that we would start a sort of 'post-a-cat' crusade - not possible though a letter box, but very possible through this woman's cellar grate. We all agreed that we'd need to post not one cat, but as many as possible.

Martin Street, and those adjoining it, had moggies in abundance. To us, they always looked a bit bored and fed up and it never entered our heads that using them for this particular prank could possibly be cruel. In fact, we thought we'd be doing them a favour by getting them all together in one place, reasoning that they'd have plenty of company, equivalent to a night out at the pub for grown-ups. We knew that we could control the time of their release, too - it wasn't like poor old Topsy's tortuous experience of inadvertent solitary confinement for several days.

We first checked that the cellar grate was not chained down. It wasn't. After that, it was plain sailing. We decided that, as cats sometimes scratch, we would each have a cardboard box for carrying our moggies. Off we went to the corner shop, 'Fletchers'.

' 'Ave ya got four cardboard boxes wi' lids on for me mam?' I asked Mr Fletcher. 'What d'ya want 'em for?' 'Wi flittin',' I lied in panic, his question catching me by surprise. 'Me mam wants 'em fot knives and forks.' (Which was a bit rich as we only had four of each.) 'Bleedin' 'ell!' he said, 'Yu've got sum stuff in your house.' Anyway, he duly obliged with the boxes and we were in business.

We began to comb Martin Street and beyond, collecting moggies one at a time. I stipulated that we would split up. It would be quicker. I also asked that our Topsy be excused involvement, being one of the family - and having suffered the torture of her previous accidental incarceration. We agreed to meet at the top of Martin Street when we each had posted five moggies. I quickly posted four and was struggling for a fifth, when old Topsy came rubbing herself around my legs. I looked at her repentantly. 'Sorry, Topsy.' Quick as a flash she was in my box and, just as quickly, she was down the cellar grate.

We all met up as arranged. I was the last, so it meant four times five, equalled twenty moggies, all nice and cosy down Mrs Miserableget's cellar.

We decided to let the moggies stew all night, knowing that the next morning we would have to devise a plan to get the woman to open her cellar door. We went home to sleep on it.

The next day, we got together and Dennis said that one of us would have to knock on Mrs Miserableget's door and, in an angelic voice, say, 'Excuse me, Missis, Ah think Ah 'eard a cat down yor cella'.' We put it to the vote and Little Pete got the job. Being the smallest, the sweetest-looking, and first reserve of the gang, he was perfect for the role.

Little Pete walked over to the door and knocked. No answer. He looked round at us, we were directly opposite on the other side of the road. We all waved our arms and mimed, 'Go on!' So he knocked again. This time the door opened, but it wasn't Mrs Miserableget. It was her husband. He looked worse than her. They seemed an ideally suited couple. He had the look of Mrs Miserableget with muscles.

'What's tha knockin' at?' he bawled at Pete. I'm sure if it had been one of the rest of us, we'd have done a runner, but Little Pete, who was desperate to be accepted as a fully-fledged member of LDV, stuck his ground. He was also word-perfect.

'Ah'm sorry for disturbin' ya, but Ah can 'ear a cat dahn yor cella'.'
'What tha talkin' abaht? We 'ant gorra cat.'

The door was wide open and we saw Mr Miserableget saunter to the cellar door. We could see Mrs Miserableget having her morning tea and, also, our ball perched on the sideboard.

He opened the cellar door and those twenty moggies shot out screeching and squealing - some across the table, some up the walls, up the curtains - all in a frightening chaos. Mrs Miserableget came dashing into the street, screaming her head off, while her husband was pulling cats off his shoulders.

We all legged it and agreed that it had all been worthwhile. If only she'd given us our ball back.

Around about this time, we had a set of routine capers. Like, for instance, if ever we saw someone on a roof, mending slates, we'd take the ladder as far away as possible, leaving Mr Roofer stranded. There were many tried and trusted ways of lightening the day. But now and again a really wonderful opportunity presented itself to us and the desire to succumb to temptation was irresistible.

Like the time when a bloke on Martin Street had been painting his drainpipe with black paint. He left his paint and brush outside while he popped inside to get something, so we borrowed them. We lifted up Little Pete, who then painted out the large, white 'mind your head' warning slash on the roof of our entry.

Later on, during the evening, I'd forgotten all about this, and was sitting in the house twiddling my thumbs and wondering what to apply myself to, when I heard a dull thud, followed by an, 'Oh, fuckin' 'ell!' On hearing this, my dad jumped up and shouted to our injured visitor, 'Who's fuckin' swearin'? Dun't tha no thiz kids and wimmin int fuckin' yard? Watch thi fuckin' language will tha?'

A distant voice said, 'Oh, sorry, Fred, Ah've banged mi chuffin' eard'.

My dad was strict about anyone swearing in front of his family.

Chapter 4

Errands

In those days, shopping was done on a day-to-day basis. No supermarkets or trolley-loads of food. You bought something to eat and ate it the same day.

Often, we'd all be playing football in our yard when my mother would shout, 'Freddie, go tut shops.' I'd think,'Chuffin' 'ell,' but it wouldn't cross my mind to grumble. You did what you were told in those days. Invariably, this would happen right in the middle of an England versus Scotland match with someone doing a running commentary: 'Mathews to Mannion, he passes to Finney, he crosses the ball and Lawton rams it into the net.' Then everyone would cheer. My mother would give me a list and a shopping bag with exactly the correct money - you knew the price of everything in those days. So, with the commentator saying, 'Oh, I think Lawton's going off injured,' to explain my absence, I'd set off. Routinely, she'd shout me back with the dreaded words, '… and go and see if Missis Smith wants owt'.

Now, Mrs Smith was an old age pensioner, over the wall from us, who was treated with the greatest respect. But I was scared to death of her, not because she was nasty - she was a nice old lady - but her appearance was particularly scary to a little kid. On these occasions, she always went through exactly the same routine. I would knock on the door, she'd shout, 'Come in,' and I'd go into a house that was in almost complete darkness. She'd have a black crocheted shawl over her head and I'd be able to see her face only dimly, by the flickering of her hardly-lit fire. The coldness and darkness of the house illustrated just how short money was in the 1940s for old ladies like her.

Then the routine started. She'd say, 'Who is it?' peer at me and follow up with, 'Oh, it's you, Freddie. Come closer. Ooo, you are getting a big lad.' I'd think, 'Bloody 'ell, there's an international match goin' on and I'm stood 'ere like a chuff … and if she dunt 'erry up, Ah'll be a lot bigger soon.'

'Do ya want owt fromt shops, Missis Smith?'
'Oh, you are a good lad, but no, love, Ah think Ah'm all reight. But thanks for callin'.'
'It's OK, Missis Smith.'

I would then turn to the door, just get my hand on the sneck and she'd say,

'Which shops are you goin' to?'
'Albion Street.'
'Ya couldn't go to Meadow Street, could ya?'
'Course Ah will.' (Thinking, 'Bloody 'ell, Albion Street's due north, Meadow Street's due south, match'll be o'er bit time Ah get back.')
"Ave a look int sideboard drawer (pointing with her spindly fingers). Ah think you'll find a pencil.'

Well, in this drawer there were bits of cotton wool, mousetraps, false teeth, old cotton bobbins, old washers, screws, in fact everything under the sun except pencils. After what seemed like an age, I'd find one about an inch long and give it to her. She'd then get a piece of paper from under the cushion she was sitting on and say, 'Ah think Ah only want a packet of dried peas,' adding, 'Oh, and ya can get me a loaf?' She'd write down what she wanted and, alongside, where from. By the time she'd done, I was fetching more for her than I was for my mother. All the time this was going on, so was the commentary for our international match, the latest comment being, 'Lawton is still off injured. I was. I was suffering from a bout of erranditis. 'Will he get back before the game's over?' I thought, 'At this rate, no chuffin' chance.'

As soon as I had the money and list, I was off in a flash. I'd decide to go down Martin Street, to avoid Black Bruce, the big black dog who hated me, onto Meadow Street, a full circle round to Bromley Street, then back home to Wembley. While on these little shopping trips, if ever I had a bag with a flower on it, or something similarly potentially embarrassing, you can bet I'd bump into a group of kids who'd call out, 'Oooo, Freddie's goin' shoppin' for iz mam.' I'd retort with a sharp, 'Fuck off,' then they'd all chase me, but not catch me, because I'd be too motivated to get away and return to our on-going international match - where England was a man short.

Mission completed, I'd dash back into the game. The commentator would shout, 'Lawton's back on for England.' About five minutes later my mother would shout, 'Freddie, cum and get thi tea.' After all that, I'd trudge into the house with the words 'Lawton's off injured again' ringing in my ears. That would seal the fate of my promising career with England. For that day, anyway.

Perhaps the errand I liked least was fetching coke, or 'cowks', from a fuel depot which belonged to the gas company. When the word went around that there would be cowks available, people used to queue up the day before to buy a ticket, which they could use the next day to claim a quarter of a hundredweight of the much sought-after fuel. The tickets went on sale on a first-come, first-served basis. 8.00am was the designated time so, by 7.30am on the day, there would be a queue like those for cup final tickets.

They went on sale at the gas depot 'gas house' on Parkwood Road, so my mother would be queuing from well before 8.00am. I was too small to leave behind, so I'd have to go with her. Getting up in winter-time before dawn and walking a mile to stand in the queue for ages, in the bitter cold, was something I hated. After standing there, frozen stiff, for what seemed like days not hours, we'd walk back with the coveted ticket to a pot of tea and a slice of toast. Then I'd be off to Crooksmoor School.

The next day I'd be up early again to be one of a wagon train of kids equipped with all sorts of makeshift vehicles in which to carry home the cowks.

I was lucky. We had a homemade barrow of sorts which, compared to those of the others, was a de-luxe removal vehicle. Some kids had to suffer the indignity of having to use an old, dilapidated high-slung pram. Others used sledges, which was great if there was snow on the ground. But no snow with a sledge meant a hard, slow, painstaking journey.

The gas house, or 'cowk' house, whichever you want to call it, would have made a perfect set for any film depicting the end of the world. Sky-high steel chimneys bellowed out clouds of goodness-knows what. Ear-splitting hisses. Little was I to know that within a few years, I would be living within sight of old Armageddon.

Anyway, we'd be off for our cowks before dawn, so that we'd be back in time for school. All my pals made the pilgrimage, too. About four or five of us would try to make a game of it and race each other to the cowk house. The big iron gates would open and, one by one, people, mainly kids, would be served, shuffling forward bit by bit. When it came to your turn, you'd see a mountain of cowks and a bloke with a huge fork. He'd snatch your ticket - they'd be like those you used to get at the pictures, the ones with a hole in the middle which made them easy to tear in half - then he'd fork cowks into a steel scoop-shaped object behind which was a big dial displaying the weight. When it showed a quarter of a hundredweight he'd shout, 'Owd di bag.' You'd hold open your sack, he'd pour in your cowks, then shout 'Next!' His attitude told you that his job wasn't exactly like picking cherries.

We would all then do our best to race back to Martin Street. Many a time, we'd get back, then Dennis, or I, would say, 'Let's 'elp owd Bert' (or anyone else from Martin Street who was unlucky enough to be using a dreaded sledge for the collection), so we'd back-track and give our pal a pull with his sledge. We all silently acknowledged that any one of us could, one day, end up being a sledge-puller.

Back home, after a pot of tea, a slice of toast and an, 'Oh, you are a good lad,' from our mothers, we'd dash off to school to be just in time for assembly, and to sing our lungs out to something like, 'We thank thee for the beauty of the Earth and the love which over and about us lies.'

Chapter 5

Ablutions

The toilet facilities in our yard consisted of six toilets - three facing the Hoggs and three facing the Aistrops. Even the toilets were back-to-back. Come to think of it, the only thing that wasn't were the people, otherwise there wouldn't have been all those kids.

Six toilets and seven houses sounds OK, but those six toilets, or closets, as we called them, not only served us, but about a dozen other houses on Martin Street. We were lucky that the toilet we used was in our yard. Pretty cushy, eh? Anyway, these toilets were used so much that they were never locked, although we did have a key. I can testify to this, because my mother once dropped it down the back of my shirt when I had a nosebleed. It was, or seemed like, about ten inches long and two pound in weight and felt like a cellar grate being dropped down my back. The key-dropping exercise was an old wives remedy. I can't say it ever worked and I wonder who thought that one up. Unless the logic was key down back equals fit, equals convulsions, equals stroke, equals loss of speech, equals, 'Has it stopped?' followed by no reply, equals 'Yes, it's worked.'

As a kid, I hated those toilets if I had to go for a pee. Because the door was never locked, you peed flamingo-style on one leg, while the sole of your non-standing foot held the door closed. If you watched any men or lads coming out, they invariably had a wet foot, due to wobbling about while trying to keep their balance. I hated going to do 'the other' because, with all those people using the toilet, the seat was always uncomfortably warm. As for the en-suite set-up we had in our bedroom, it was a bucket.

Friday night was one night that held trepidation for me, for Friday night was bath night. Filling the bath was a long, laborious grind for my mother. She'd boil water on the fire and on the gas ring, and then use anything that held water to fill the bath. There would always be a big roaring fire. The tin bath, which hung at the back of our cellar door, would be placed in front of the fire. The procedure was that my mother would bath me, put me to bed, and then go and have a natter with Mrs Aistrop, while my brother, who was a teenager, then bathed in the same water.

So, what with the fire, steam, and the water temperature, bath night was not something I looked forward to. I tried all the dodges to avoid it. My mother would shout me in and the conversation went something like:

'Weerz me dad?'
'Ya know iz at work.'
'Ah've 'urt mi leg '
'It'll feel better when tha'z 'ad di bath.'
'Ah feel sick.'
'Ya will feel sick soon, lad.'
'Ah'm not mucky.'
'Tha'll not be in five minits.'
'Dennis Aistrop dunt get bathed.'
'Well you are, mi lad.'

So, I would lower myself into the bath, reluctantly resigned to my fate, then stand up while my mother washed me, armed with a block of soap. And that was another thing. It was about the size of half a brick, it had sharp corners and was about as subtle. Two names spring to mind, two inappropriate names if ever there were. Mother Shipton's and Fairy.

Friday night was payday, so my bath was usually interrupted by some credit collector, who would knock and walk in. His greeting was usually something like, 'Evening, love, Wigfalls,' or whatever company he represented.

These blokes, choose what the weather, wore big gabardine raincoats with a belt fastened just under the armpits. Gabardine raincoats were a sort of uniform for plain-clothes police in those days, which was daft because, by dressing in a gabardine raincoat, you told everyone that you were a copper. Trying to emulate their status, collectors also wore them, mistakenly thinking they gave them an air of authority. They also always wore a permanent smile. I don't know why they bothered, no one on Martin Street was pleased to see them.

'It's ont' sideboard,' my mother would say curtly, referring to his payment. Then, while dotting down the details in his book, he'd say something gormless like, 'Avin' ya Friday bath then, Freddie.' And I, sensing my mother's indifference to him, wouldn't reply, but would be thinking of a choice rebuke, his comment confirming that you didn't need brains to be a debt collector up Martin Street. Just nerves of steel and a skin as thick as a rhino'.

These collectors would always leave the door ajar while

conducting their business, so I invariably got a stiff breeze up my arse, solely because I always kept my back to these blokes. I didn't want any Wigfalls bloke seeing my twiddly bits.

The bathing would close with my mother saying, 'Close yor eyes while Ah rinse yor 'air.' Then, using a big pint pot, she'd pour about half a dozen pots of bath water over my head, after which she'd dry me down with a towel, which was an experience in itself. All our towels were of the 'no pile' variety. It was like being dried with a sack.

She'd comb my hair, put me a clean shirt on, and say, 'Up them apples and pears, love,' followed by the classic, 'Ah bet ya feel a lot better nah.'

I was usually too weak to answer, but I was always glad there was only one Friday night in a week.

Chapter 6

Wireless Days

In the middle and late '40s we had the ultimate in entertainment, a wireless. Ours was about as big as a beer crate and, for some reason, my dad had put it up high on the wall on a homemade shelf. My first recollections were of listening to it before setting off for school.

One particular programme sticks in my mind, 'The Radio Doctor'. I'd be sitting there in front of the fire, on dark mornings, shivering, with a pot of tea in my hands, listening to this doctor going on about the symptoms of various illnesses. He'd start by saying something like, 'Good morning, listeners. Today our subject is mumps.' I'd think, 'Nowt like getting t'day off to a good start.'

Sometimes I'd memorise the symptoms and use them for a day off school. My mother fell for my little ruse a few times and would whisk me off to old Dr Rigby's.

I used to hate going to Dr Rigby's surgery on St Phillips Road. At one time, it had been a shop and the large windows, which faced the street, were painted halfway up in a dark brown colour. In the waiting room, was a circle of chairs, and the room was lit centrally by a single light bulb, which hung forlornly on a plaited, dark, electrical cord.

The waiting room was always packed and, sometimes, you'd have to stand for half an hour before you'd get a seat. Little kids mostly didn't ever get seats. It would have been unthinkable to see a child sitting while a grown up was standing.

Waiting for what seemed like hours was a nightmare. What was worse, was the smoke because most people were quietly puffing away on untipped cigarettes. But, all in all, I felt that it was worth it, if it meant getting a couple of days off school.

Eventually I'd be ushered by my mother into the surgery where I'd describe the symptoms to Dr Rigby and he'd say something along the lines of, 'It sounds like mumps to me, Mrs Pass. I should keep him off school for a couple of days, just in case.'

Unfortunately, occasionally, the doctor on the radio would feature more unusual diseases. So my ruse was sussed once and for all when, one day, my mother took me off to Doc Rigby's and I told him my symptoms. After some consideration, he turned to my mother. 'This may sound preposterous, Mrs Pass, but your Freddie has the classic symptoms of blackwater fever, which is only prevalent in Outer Mongolia - or other places a million miles from Martin Street.'

It suddenly clicked with my mother, and she jumped up quickly. 'Sorry for wasting your time, Doctor.' Old Doc Rigby looked astonished. He'd just about managed a couple of 'buts' before we were out of his surgery. On getting outside, I asked, 'Where we going, mam?' Her retort was unambiguous. 'Ah know where you're goin', mi lad. School. And if thee ever tries owt like that agee'rn, *he'll* get to know,' referring to my dad.

The final thing I'd hear on the wireless, before leaving the house in the morning, was the shipping forecast. Some bloke would start on about fisher, dogger, bite and the like. When I asked my mother why they gave out shipping forecasts on Martin Street when I'd never even seen a ship, she told me it was for fishermen who were listening to the wireless while out at sea.

I didn't pursue my questioning of my mother. Mornings were never a good time. But, as a kid, I thought that if I was on a ship I'd have a rough idea if I was in a force ten gale or not. I had this picture in my head of a little boat getting tossed all over the place, while all the seamen were huddled around a wireless saying, 'Shurrup, weather forecast's on.'

Thinking about it, there was a range of programmes on the radio which defied understanding. There were also some which fascinated and entertained.

One of the former was 'The Archie Andrews Show', starring Peter Brough, the ventriloquist, and his dummy, Archie Andrews. Peter Brough must have had the best job in show business, when you stop and think. A ventriloquist on the radio. No one was going to see his lips move, no matter how hard they tried.

'Carol Levis's Discoveries' was another. That was a talent show and one week a magician won it. All we got was a bloke describing his tricks. Anyway, when this magician was announced the winner, my mother said something like, 'Ooo, Ah bet ee were good,' as we all sat round staring at the wireless, which, for some reason, we always did - something else that defied logic.

Then there was 'Have a go' with Wilfred Pickles, Violet Carson and Barney Somebody-or-other. The climax of the show was someone answering questions for the jackpot. Wilfred Pickles would say, 'What's in the jack-pot tonight then, Barney?' and Barney would say something like, 'Half a dozen eggs, a packet of tea, a pound of flour and seventeen shillings and fourpence,' at which the studio audience would exclaim in unison 'Ooooo!', amazed that anyone could have such good fortune. If anyone won, you'd think, 'Lucky sod.' Hardly 'Who wants to be a millionaire.' The programme would end to the tune of 'Have a go, Joe, your mother doesn't know' and rapturous applause from the studio audience.

One show which used to give me the shivers was a programme presented by Valentine Dyall, who would introduce it with the words, 'My name is Valentine Dyall. I am the man in black.' Then, there'd be noises like the howling of the wind and the creaking of a door and I'd sit there, listening, with my elbows on the table, holding my chin in the palm of my hands, looking up at the radio, thinking, 'Chuffin' 'ell.' Valentine would then set the scene for what turned out to be a mystery play.

I'd listen intently, as the play unfolded, to the sound effects of someone running on gravely paths, doors slamming, screams and all that sort of stuff. It was terrific exercise for your imagination. And Valentine Dyall had a rich, deep voice - perfect for radio.

Finally, there was 'The Lost World', a programme about a group of travellers who, somehow or other, had landed on a strange planet. There was, at the start of the serial, a group of about eight people. A couple of them seemed disagreeable and one had a German accent. I knew, even as a little kid that, any mishap, and he'd be the first to go.

Sure enough, you'd hear grumbling while he cut a path for himself through a jungle. Then there'd be a blood-curdling roar, then a scream, then bone-crunching noises … and it was exit Hans. You were left to imagine whatever you wanted as to what the monster looked like.

One particular morning, I'd been listening to 'The Doctor' (who, by the way, always sounded bunged-up with a cold. I used to think 'I bet he never gets time to go to the doctor's himself, being on the radio all the time') going on about the fun of having rabies or something, followed by gale warnings on Dogger Bank, before setting off for school.

I was hardly full of the joys of spring, when I bumped into Bert Marples, a pal of mine who lived on Martin Street. Bert suggested that we give school a miss and go down to town to the rag 'n' tag market to look at the pups and such like in the pet shop there. I had to think for a full second before I agreed. It was either a day with our teacher, who had a face like a well-kept grave, or a day in the market. No contest. Off we went.

The market was a wondrous place for little kids. We had a set pattern of operation. We'd watch people get weighed, see the pets, mooch around, nick an apple or so and, generally, get up to no good.

We'd be entertained by old Potty Edwards, banging and rattling his plates without breaking them, and the weighing scales were always a good source of amusement. I, and whoever was with me, would hide behind old boxes at the back of the scales. When a fat woman got on, we'd shout 'Ger-off!' just as she sat on the scales, then dash off before the bloke with the scales gave us a clip.

Anyway, this particular day, as we entered the market, there was a bloke ranting on about some stuff he was trying to sell. It was little bottles of black, thick stuff and was supposed to cure, among other things, baldness, piles, rheumatics and corns. To get people to stop and listen to his patter, he performed magic tricks, so, on seeing this, we pushed to the front. He was performing a trick involving four silver rings. He held them up to show that they were separate, then juggled them around a bit and declared, 'Wallah!' As if by magic all the rings joined up, with us two thinking, 'Bleedin' 'ell, arz 'e do it?'

Eventually, we both trudged home, agreeing that we'd had a smashing day and that we'd go again the following week. I got home and no one was the wiser but, a couple of days later, on returning from school, I was greeted by my mother holding a copy of 'The Sheffield Star' in her hand.

"Ave ya seen this lot?'

'What lot?'

'That lot.' (Pointing to a picture of Bert and me looking up at this bloke with the rings.)

'What do ya mean?' (Looking at every part of the page, except the picture.)

'That chuffin' lot.' (Pointing more emphatically at the picture.)

'Oooo, dunt that look like Bert Marples.'

'And dunt that look like bleedin' thee!'

'Oh, Ah suppose it does really.'

'Caption underneath is best: "Two young chaps bewildered by the mysteries of life". On'y chuffin' mystery is what were ya doin' int chuffin' market when ya shudda been at school. All't bleedin' street'll know. What they gonna think of us, if teachers see it? Tha'll end up int 'omes, mi lad, if ya don't change ya ways. I dern't tell thi dad. 'E'll bleedin' kill thee. Ya keep away fromt markets, ya keep away from bleedin' Bert Marples and (the final crushing blow) ya not goin' to Auntie May's on Sunday.

I tried to slip into my 'I'm not very well' routine, but it fell on deaf ears. I was confined to the house, listening to my mother going on and on, while I sat there, looking suitably chastised, but thinking, 'I wonder what that monster looks like in The Lost World?'

Chapter 7

Whit Sunday

Bert and I on our own were probably okay. But put the two of us together and it usually meant disaster. I particularly remember one Whit Sunday.

I used to hate Whit Sundays. Your mother would get you all dressed up in new clothes, including a tie (which was the only time you ever wore one) and send you on your way to visit various members of your family. You'd visit all conceivable relatives, some who hardly recognised you, and they'd say something like, 'Oh, ya do look nice, Freddie,' or 'Ooo, you 'ave shot up.' You'd smile sweetly in response, while thinking, 'Just give me some money and let me piss off.' After traipsing all over Sheffield visiting long-lost relatives, who were about as pleased to see you as you were to see them, the end product was about seventeen and a tanner, which you'd give to your mother, and out of which she'd give you back two bob.

Well, this particular Whit Sunday, Bert and I decided to join forces and visit each other's relatives, thinking that twice the number of relatives equalled twice the money.

So, after my mother had sent me off with a warning not to play football in my brand new shoes, Bert and I began our pilgrimage to raise serious cash.

We'd only been in the road five minutes, when a ball came rolling down the street with some kids following, shouting, 'That ball.' Despite the warning from my mother, I casually kicked the ball back. Big mistake. While kicking the ball, I also kicked the ground, ripping part of the sole loose from the rest of my shoe. The result was a less-than-perfect shoe, which made a sort of 'flip-flop' noise as I walked. Reliving the sight of my mother's face seriously issuing the shoe warning, I knew that, choose what, I'd be in trouble when I got home.

From then on, as we did our rounds, beside the usual, 'Oh, ya do look nice,' I got an added, 'What ya dun to ya shoe?' which, on each visit we paid, further compounded my fears of facing mother.

Then I had a brain wave. I remembered my dad saying that my Uncle Jack had never brought back some fishing tackle that he'd borrowed so, when I got to Uncle Jack's, I said, 'Oh, me dad sez 'as tha dun wit fishin' tackle?' The result was that I came away with a tanner plus a fishing basket and rod. It was a burden I was willing to carry to redress the damage done to my shoe and made me much more confident about going back home.

By this time I was beginning to look rather odd. On giving me the fishing tackle, Uncle Jack had also given me one of my dad's flat caps that he'd also once borrowed. So, there I was, with my dad's cap on, carrying a fishing rod and basket and wearing a flapping shoe.

In between visits to relatives, Bert kept going on about how it wasn't fair that we'd do all the walking about and end up with just two bob. He also said that if we spent a bit no one would be the wiser. In the end, after a while of Bert's going on, and with the last relative thoroughly visited, we decided we'd spend a bit and 'sey nowt'.

With sweets - commonly known as 'spice' to us at that time - being on ration, we were limited, but we managed to buy dates, figs, grapes, pop and all sorts of stuff. The results were disastrous. After about half an hour, I had a burning in my stomach and my arse felt on fire. Suddenly, I lost control of the battle raging inside me and felt diarrhoea flow down my legs.

At this, Bert started laughing. In my attempts to mop up the diarrhoea with some paper, I got the stuff all over my hands, which sent Bert into more intense paroxysms of mirth. So I smeared some on his new shirt. That stopped him laughing. But, what with the cocktail of foods he'd consumed and the sudden close proximity of the awful smell, Bert was promptly sick all over himself and ran off shouting abuse.

On getting home, I walked down the entry of our yard. With my shoe flipping and flopping, a flat cap on (six sizes too big), a long fishing rod in my hand and a large fishing basket on my shoulder, covered in shit and with about one and nine in my pocket instead of fifteen bob.

My mother was chatting in the yard to a group of neighbours. 'Ah've got me dad's fishin' tackle,' I shouted, at which they all turned around. At the sight of me they just stood there with open mouths, quietly taking in the scene for what seemed like ages. Mrs Aistrop broke the silence eventually. 'Fuckin' 'ell,' she said, under her breath.

Chapter 8

This 'n' that

During the six weeks' holiday, I could always tell when I was beginning to get on my mother's nerves. I'd dash into the house and the conversation I had with her would make no sense at all.

'Weerz me dad?'

'Tha'll get, 'Weerz me dad''

'Weer iz 'e then?'

'Weerz tha think 'e iz?'

'Ah dunt 'no'.'

'Ah've 'ad abaht enough of this lot.'

'What lot?'

'Tha'll get, 'What lot'.'

'What's up?'

'What's up? What's up? 'E'll get to 'no' abaht this lot.'

'Who?'

'Thi dad. Who's tha think?'

'Weer iz 'e then?'

This mind-boggling exchange would end up by her saying, 'Get out a this chuffin' 'ouse. Tha drives me mad mitherin' all t'time.' I'd dash out shell-shocked and puzzled.

One day, I was sitting on a corner of Martin Street, listening to the older boys talking, saying, 'I've 'ad a good shag, I've shagged 'er,' and so on. 'What's a shag?' I asked one of them. This sparked intense amusement and they started to take the mickey.

'Oh, little Passey dunt 'no' what a shag is.' 'Yes, I do.' 'Go on then, tell us,' they challenged. At this, I removed myself a suitable distance and shouted, 'Fuck off. My feyther can feight tha feyther any day,' which had nowt to do with owt, but seemed, at the time, a suitable retaliation.

I dashed off, but knew that I had to find the meaning of this new word as soon as possible, mainly because, inevitably, I'd bump into them again before too long and they'd taunt, 'Come on then, Passey, what's a shag?'

My Auntie May had always told me, 'It's good to ask questions. It's the only way you learn owt.' So, I marched into the house where my mother was ironing away, listening to workers' playtime. 'Mam, what's a shag?'

She went ballistic. 'You 'orrible little bugger. Ah'll cut thi tong out if tha ever sez that word in this house agee'rn.'

She'd got the iron in her hand at the time, so I dashed outside and made myself scarce for a couple of hours or so, thinking, 'Chuffin' 'ell, she's in one of her bad moods agee'rn.'

I got back in the house at teatime. The iron might have cooled down, but she hadn't.

'Ya 'no' thee, tha'll end up int' dogs' 'ome saying words like that.'
'Words like what?'
'Tha'll get, 'Words like what?' If I 'ear it agee'rn, 'e'll get to 'no'

42

about this lot.'

I just sat in silence. I didn't fancy any more, 'What lot/this lot/that lot' conversations.

Shortly after, my mother decided that Sunday School would be good for me so, for a while on Sunday mornings, Little Pete Marshall and I would trudge off to this place on Scotland Street to be bored stiff.

In all, my religious education lasted a full three weeks. And it was curtailed by me - or, should I say, the bloke in charge - when, one morning, he invited questions from all us kids. At this point in the lesson each week, I'd usually be looking through the window, while other kids would ask things like, 'How do flowers grow?' or 'Does God love us?' and stuff like that. The Sunday School teacher would attempt to answer these daft questions by going on and on while everyone was dropping off to sleep - even the kids who had asked the questions.

A couple of weeks before, he'd said he'd noticed that I'd not asked any questions and said that I must never be scared to ask anything, for God had given him the ability to answer all sorts of questions.

So, this particular week, when old Martin Luther Nuttall, or whatever he was called, asked for questions all the usual hands shot up, ready with their 'Why do birds tweet?' sort of stuff, I put my hand up. His eyes lit up. He must have thought he was finally getting me interested, so he homed in.

'Yes, you, Freddie Pass, what's your question?'

'What's a shag?'

The atmosphere changed from 'Sunday morning snooze' to 'A Night at the London Palladium' in seconds. The older kids rolled about laughing.

Well, old Martin Luther must have thought it was a deliberate action by me to embarrass him, despite the fact that, in reality, the question had been asked in all innocence. Anyway, he blew his top, telling me to go and never to return. God had obviously not prepared him for innocent questions.

I shuffled off back home, mulling it all over. 'Fuckin' 'ell, what does it mean?' I decided, then, to drop it once and for all.

My mother was surprised by my early return. 'You're soon back. What's up?' Trying not to lie, I replied, 'Sunday School teacher's not very well.' It wasn't a lie because he wasn't well the last time I saw him. He'd looked dreadful.

Pure innocence was often to the fore in my childhood experiences, invariably causing amusement for everyone but me. Like the day I was playing on 'the tip' at the top of Martin Street. Now 'The tip' was two flattened areas on two levels, each the size of a football pitch, which is what they were used for. The big lads - aged fourteen and over - used to play on the top pitch and the younger ones played on the other, which was about ten feet lower. Both were covered in cinders, hence the name ' the tip'. To you, this may not have the same ring as the 'Coca cabaña' or Wembley Stadium, but it did to us.

At the top end of the pitches was a grass slope with a winding row of steps that lead you to the main road and on to Weston Park. On the right side of the grassed area was a park-keeper's hut situated about three feet from the perimeter wall.

Anyway, this day, I'd been playing football and decided to go for a drink of water from the water fountain by the side of the park-keeper's hut. It was one of those water fountains that had a knob on the side, which you turned and water would spring up - usually up your nose.

So, there I was, having my drink, and I heard this groaning and banging noise. I looked down the side of the hut and there was this man and woman. 'Are you all right, mester?' I asked. Neither replied.

I judged from their expressions that they were in pain, and deduced that they were stuck and couldn't get out from the side of the hut. I dashed off to tell my mam. I ran into the house where she and three or four neighbours were sitting around drinking tea.

'Weerz me dad?'
'At work.'
'Mam, thiz a man 'n' woman stuck down t'side of park-keeper's hut.'

I found the reaction of my audience mildly upsetting. They burst out laughing and began to spit tea all over. Thinking I hadn't made myself clear, I repeated my plea. 'They are. Thi stuck and (holding the palms of my hands up high on my chest) the woman's

45

skirt's up here,' - which made them laugh louder. By this time, I was beside myself with frustration and began pulling at my mother's arm. 'Come on, mam, thi stuck.'

One of the women said something like, 'Ah wish Ah were,' and they laughed more. So, I tried a different angle. 'Thi both moanin' and groanin'.' 'Ah bet they are,' said my mother, triggering even louder laughter. In desperation, I added, 'They're wriggling abaht reight quick, tryin' to get out.' By this time, the laughing was at fever pitch, so I decided to throw in the towel with my parting words, 'They're not laughin'!'

I wondered back into the yard, bemused by the fact that I'd found someone in trouble and all my mother and her mates could do was laugh. Anyway, when I went to school the next day, I made a point of looking to see if the couple had got out. I breathed a sigh of relief when they were not there.

Sometimes, during the long boring days of the summer holidays, we would roam around, wondering what to do next. Sometimes, we would pester our mothers for tuppence bus fare to Endcliffe Park, then walk it there and back and spend the money on ice lollies, or owt, really. There'd be Dennis, Lawrence and me, ready to set off, when Little Pete would chime up, 'Can ah come?' We'd let him.

On one of these excursions, Pete revealed a special gift. He could cry at the drop of a hat.

Pete was smaller than us, angelic-looking and wore short, long trousers (or were they long, short trousers?) and hob-nailed boots. His socks were always rolled down.

On the day of the discovery, on our way to the Park, Pete started crying. By now, you'll have picked up that we were not an over-sensitive bunch but, nevertheless, we were sufficiently moved to cluster around him. 'What's up, Pete?' I remember my bottom lip trembling at the heart-rending scene. Then, all of a sudden, he stopped crying and laughed, 'That got ya, dinnit?'

He was a natural at crying. You see present-day actors crying on screen and you can tell that they're acting. With Pete, there was no such transparency. Suddenly, he was a worthwhile member of the gang.

So began a regular and lucrative scam. We'd get ourselves in Endcliffe Park and wait until we saw some likely, unsuspecting woman approach, preferably one with a hat, or with a handbag, or a fur coat - each one an indication of money, and Endcliffe Park was at the posh end of town, so prospects were good. When we saw a potential victim approach, we'd all shout abuse and swear at Little Pete.

'Ya little twat.' 'Ah'm gonna thump him.' 'Let me at 'im.' Little Pete would cry his heart out, pleading, 'Ah'm sorry. Ah'm sorry. Don't hit me. Please ... please!'

Then Mrs Moneybags would stop and rebuke us with, 'You leave him alone,' put her arms around him, and ask him what was the matter.

Pete would look meaningfully into her eyes and waver, 'It's my fault. Me mother gev us two bob bus fares and Ah've lost it. Please, don't let 'em 'it me.'

The woman would tighten a protective arm around Pete and coo, 'They won't hit you,' delve into her handbag, and give Pete two bob, saying, 'There you are', then leave, cursing us three as she went.

As time went on, our performances became more sophisticated. We devised a scale of requests for money - well, Pete did - carefully judged, according to the appearance of our victim. With sweets on ration, we used it to buy figs, dates, even oxo cubes - in fact anything you could suck. The LDV had grown in to the LDVC. Look, duck, vanish and cry.

The six weeks holiday always seemed a long, sprawling, hot sort of time. We were invariably bored out of our brains. One Friday, Dennis, Pete and Jenks got a few pennies together, and it was decided that a good way to pass a day would be to go to Bramall Lane to watch Yorkshire play Surrey at cricket. The one problem was that I had no money, so I approached my mam.

'Mam, can I have two bob?'

'No.'

'Why?'

'Because Ah've not got two bob.'

'Thi all gooin' tut cricket.'

'Well you're not.'

'Why?'

'Because Ah've not got two bob. Thiz a couple of bottles int' corner. Tek em back.'

'It'll not be enuff.'

'It'll 'ave to be.'

I went back outside to tell my mates that I couldn't go because I didn't have enough money. 'Go ask ya dad at work,' said Dennis, so off we went down to Neepsend. I didn't tell my mother what my solution to the cash shortage problem was. She'd have gone beserk at the thought of me asking my dad for money, especially while he was at work.

I entered the rolling mill through a big doorway. It was a terrifying place for a little kid. I had to walk into, what seemed like, complete darkness, and the noise was deafening.

Suddenly, I saw my dad. He was using a large set of tongs to drag a red hot bar of steel. He wore a vest and had a sweat towel around his neck, with one end of it stuffed in his mouth. He was dripping with sweat and his face was covered in muck. As soon as he saw me, he dropped his tongs and ran over to where I was standing.

'What ya doin' 'ere?'
'Can I go tut cricket?'
'Chuffin' cricket! What's yor mother doin' lettin' ya cum down 'ere? Ya'll get thissen bleedin' killed walkin' around in 'ere.'
She dunt 'no'.'

My dad put his hand into his pocket and gave me two shillings, adding, 'And don't forget to tell ya mother where ya goin'.'
I instantly forgot. I wasn't going to go back home and let her

find out where I got the money from. After all, I had a strong sense of self-preservation.

We reached Bramall Lane before play had started and promptly climbed over some railings that separated the cheap area from the dear area, the Pavilion. It was a beautiful sunny day, and so peaceful, listening to the bat hitting the ball, and hearing the spectators politely clapping.

My thoughts wandered back to my dad and I suddenly felt sorry for him, working in that hellhole of a rolling mill, while all the men around me were enjoying such a pleasant afternoon in a lovely setting. Although only about three miles apart, it might as well have been a million.

A bloke across from us, dressed in a blazer and striped tie, now and again clapped and, with a 'Terry Thomas' sort of accent said something like, 'Jolly good shot, old boy.' This caused us much amusement, so, every time he made a comment, we laughed out loud and mimicked him. He soon became fed up with this and left. To our horror, he returned with a bloke who was dressed in a brown smock. He was a steward, it turned out. Terry Thomas pointed us out to him and demanded, 'Throw them out!' The steward duly complied. 'Come on, lads,' and led the four of us to the gateway, which led to the street. All of a sudden, without prompting, Little Pete started to cry. The official looked down at him and then veered left and opened a gate that led back to the cheap area. Thanks to Pete, we saw the remainder of the day's play.

Throughout the match, my mind was filled with the image of my dad's working day, struggling to earn a living, while Terry

Thomas was probably eating cucumber sandwiches.

When we arrived back home, I was greeted with,

'Wher've ya been?'

'Eh?'

'Ah 'no' where ya've been. Ya've been tut cricket and ya've been to ya dad tut Hallamshire askin' for money and yu'll stop in na mi lad (and then passed the ultimate death sentence) an ya'll not go to Auntie May's on Sunday.'

Chapter 9

Granddad

My mother's dad, James Stones, was the only grandparent I ever knew. He had spent all his working life as a drayman, latterly at a brewery just round the corner from the family home on Whitehouse Lane. The outer building still stands today, as the now derelict Kelvin Metals.

The house on Whitehouse Lane was a back-to-back house. It had one room downstairs, one bedroom upstairs and then an attic. During the short time I knew him, he was retired and living with his only unmarried daughter, my Auntie May. May had spent some time working as a 'bakeress' in Blackpool, but had come back to Sheffield to look after granddad.

Granddad was a stocky sort of bloke, about five feet eight inches tall, with snow-white hair and a white moustache. He had a ruddy complexion and epitomised what an idealised granddad should look like.

I had to stay with granddad and Auntie May when my mother was taken into hospital after an accident at home. Auntie May, at the time, was working full-time at Mays the Cleaners on South Road, so I had to be left with granddad during the day.

Sometimes, Auntie May would try and organise a day out for the two of us. On one such day, she said to granddad, 'Ah know, why not take Freddie to Endcliffe Park. It will do both of you good to get out.' She gave granddad some money and said that it would cover our bus fares and there'd be enough to buy me an ice cream cornet, cautioning, 'Don't let him run off,' and, 'Watch the road,' and so on. Granddad, with his eyes fixed to mine, just nodded in acknowledgement.

Once she had gone, and hardly before the door had closed, he started. 'Just look at what Ah've come to. Chuffin' babbi sittin'. He mumbled on, 'Bleedin' babbi sittin', a drayman like me lookin' after a scrawny little bugger like thee. Ah'm respected round 'ere, tha knows. Ah knows mi 'orses inside out.'

I just sat there, listening in an uncomfortable silence. 'Bar for thee, Ah'd be int pub.' Then he gave me a warning, 'and don't start pestering 'n' mithering. Come on,' adding, as we left the house, 'chuffin' Endcliffe chuffin' Park.'

At this point, I tried to take a hold of his hand, but he brushed it aside, 'Gerroff, tha't not a tart, are tha?' As we set off, I noticed we weren't heading for the bus-stop, so I said, 'Granddad, bus-stop's that way,' 'Tha's mitherin' me nah and we ampt set off yet,' he growled back, 'Wi walkin' it. It'll do thi good.' It was obvious that he wasn't enjoying the day and this was my only consolation.

Endcliffe Park was a round trip of about four miles but, to me at the time, it seemed more like forty-four. It also took an age because granddad, every now and then, would say, "Ave a rest.' During one of these rests, I blurted out, 'Who's Noel Vale?' 'Ah don't kno', stop chuffin' mitherin'.'

At another stop he said, 'Ah wish tha'd been my lad, Fred. Dost thi kno' why?' 'Why, granddad?' I asked. 'Because, Ah'd 'ave drowned thee at birth,' he retorted, chuckling to himself.

Despite his blatant animosity, I wasn't scared of him. Most of the time, while he talked to me, I just switched off in total indifference. When we arrived at the park, I got a tennis ball out of my top pocket and rushed around kicking the life out of it, while he sat on a form, watching. After a while, he shouted me over, 'Come an' sit dahn a bit, tha't meckin' me badly, tha't dashing abaht like someone not reight.'

After sitting a while next to him, my mind wondered to my mother in hospital, and to a time a week or two before when she was crying. I suddenly burst out crying too. Granddad looked at me bemused, 'Chuffin' 'ell, what's wrong with thee nah?' 'Iz mi mam gonna die, granddad?' 'Don't talk so chuffin' daft, ya soft chuff 'n' stop cryin'. People will think wi not reight int 'eard,' then mumbled, 'Roorin' bleedin' kids, that's all Ah want.' To me, he added, 'Thi mother's not goin' to dee, she'll be aht ot 'ospital before tha can say Jack Robinson.'

He didn't go on to reassure me that my mother wouldn't die, but gave me his philosophy of dying, the niceties of dying, if you like. He explained, 'It's only like somebody switching lights out, when tha dees.' He pointed to a tree, saying, 'Tha sees them leaves ont tree? They're alive.' He then picked up a dead leaf and said, 'This one's dee'ed,' and went on, 'This one dees and another grows in its place, and we're just the same.'

To placate me, he gave me a penny, saying, "Ere, tha can get a penny lollipop ont way 'ome.' The ice-cream that Auntie May had told him to get me had suddenly turned into a penny lolly. This generous gesture was his attempt to cheer me up.

So, there I was, sitting with my granddad, my cheeks soaked in tears. People occasionally walked by and smiled warmly for we must have looked like the perfect granddad-grandson combination.

Granddad suddenly said, 'Chuff 'em all 'xept me and thee, Fred, lad. What's tha say?' 'Aye, granddad,' I replied. He chuckled and added, ''n' chuff thee an' all.'

Absent-mindedly, I began sucking the penny he'd given me. He suddenly saw what I was doing. 'Tha'll be in trouble if tha swallows that. Tha's seen ar people get money arght o' money boxes, ant tha? If tha swallows it, Ah'll 'ave to pick thee up whit neck and shove a knife up thi arse to work it arght.' Well, that stopped me putting money into my mouth ever again.

I got my lolly on the way back to Whitehouse Lane and, on one of our rests, I asked again,

'Are ya sure ya don't 'no' Noel Vale, granddad?'
'Shurrup abaht Noel bleedin' Vale.'
'Doctor 'no's 'im.'
'Well, ask doctor, then. I've never 'erd orrim.'

We got back to the house just before Auntie May got home from work. When she arrived, she asked the predictable question, 'Well, have you two had a good day. Granddad had his eyes fixed to mine and, before I could say anything, answered, 'Smashin'. It's been smashing.' 'Did you get the bus OK?' she asked. Quick as a flash, he was there again. 'Spot on.' She then turned to me. 'And did

55

you have a nice ice-cream cornet, Freddie?' I didn't bother trying to open my mouth. It was a waste of time. "E's 'ad the biggest cornet tha's ever seen, ant tha, Fred, lad?' 'Ay,' I replied. She then asked, 'Has he been any trouble, then?' (She would have been better asking me the question about him.) 'Good as gold. No trouble at all, but he keeps on about a bloke called Noel Vale. Do you 'no' anyone called that?' She looked at me quizzically, then granddad chimed up, 'Come on then, lass, get tea on.' She'd hardly got her coat off, but within minutes was preparing a meal for the three of us.

Afterwards, she suggested that granddad went for a pint. He said that he had no money, knowing full well that she'd give him a couple of bob to get rid of him for an hour or so.

Once he'd gone, the house seemed a different place. 'Who's this person you keep asking about? Is someone bullying you?' 'No, I replied, 'Well, don't look so worried,' she said, 'Where have you got the name from?'

So I told her about the time a couple of weeks before when my mother had sent for Dr Rigby. He examined me and I heard him say to my mother, 'I really don't know how you live in these conditions. I have written countless letters to Noel Vale.'

What upset me was when the doctor left the house. I noticed a tear running down my mother's cheek and, as she was wiping it away, I said, 'Who's Noel Vale?' She laughed through the tears and said, 'No-one for you to worry about, love.'

But I did worry. I kept thinking, 'Who's this bloke Noel Vale, who's making my mother cry?' Auntie May then went to great lengths to explain that the doctor was trying his best to get us rehoused, but nothing had come of it and that that was called doing something 'to no avail'.

I didn't know my granddad for much longer. He died when I was about seven. I got home from school one day and Mrs Aistrop told me that my mother was at my Auntie May's. I ran round to find no-one downstairs, but I could hear noises coming from upstairs. I crept up the stairs to see my granddad, lying in bed, with his head out at one side, spewing blood into a bucket. My mother and Auntie May had blood all over their aprons. They didn't notice me, but granddad did. While he couldn't speak, he indicated by pointing to me. I stood staring at this horrible sight. My mother quickly ushered me downstairs with instructions to go home, saying that she wouldn't be long.

Granddad died of cancer a couple of days or so later. You could say his description of dying, 'like someone switching the lights off,' was a bit off the mark, judging by what I'd seen that night in his bedroom. He was buried in Wardsend Cemetery, on a hillside, overlooking Owlerton dog track, in the same grave as my grandmother, whom I never knew. I wasn't particularly upset because he didn't mean anything to me. I didn't know him that well and, to a little kid, a funeral is a non-event. But something strange did happen at the funeral.

It sounds so melodramatic, that I hesitate before writing it. A railway line ran behind the cemetery and, as they were lowering granddad down the hole, a leaf blew onto the top of the coffin. At the same time a train sped past, sounding its whistle. The two things together made my hair stand on end.

Funerals were about the only time that the family was together: Auntie May, Auntie Annie, Auntie Elsie, Auntie Alice, my mother and her brothers, Uncle Jim and Uncle Tom. In the years that followed his death, I spent many an hour discussing granddad with my mother and they gave me a good insight into the man's character and values.

She said that granddad always grumbled about having five daughters because girls were relatively low earners, compared to boys. He was also very strict. She told me that, one night, Auntie Alice came home at ten past ten, when she'd been told to be home for ten on the dot. She found that he'd packed her bags. He threw her out. Aged nineteen, with nowhere to go, she ended up working in her auntie's chip shop on Langsett Road, facing the Unity picture house. For working five dinner times and five nights in the chip shop, she received her food and lodgings. Despite the pleas of my grandmother, he would not have her in the house again.

My mother said that he'd come home the worse for drink and any ensuing argument would end up with him hitting my grandmother. My mother said that she and her brothers and sisters used to take it in turns to fetch the local bobby from the police station on Langsett Road. My grandmother was said to have weighed no more than six stone, wet through, which says a lot.

My mother told me that, on her death, granddad had said that grandmother wasn't insured so she'd have to have a pauper's funeral. My grandmother's maiden name had been Wragg (she was a relation of the famous old jockey, Harry Wragg) and granddad assumed that her family would fund the funeral. As it turned out, they wouldn't, so the cost was met by all his children clubbing together. My mother sold our sideboard. All the rest of the family raised the money in similar ways, in what were very hard times. Granddad even accepted money from Auntie Alice, who he still considered an outcast.

After he'd died, my mother found out that he had, indeed, had grandmother insured, but had kept the money to himself.

Despite all this, granddad, both before and after his death, was still held in great respect by his family. I asked my mother how they could respect him, when he'd acted the way he did. All I could get out of her was, 'It was the way things were.'

Chapter 10

Heroes and Villains

The first local bloke, other than members of my family, to turn out to be a hero in my eyes was Roger Taylor, the international tennis star. Roger and I started at Crooksmoor School at the same time and, while I knew him well, he didn't knock around with us. It may seem silly but, even as a little lad, he had an aura about him that screamed out that he was going to turn out something special. Roger was a big, dark-haired, good-looking kid who seemed to do everything left-sided. He kicked a football with his left foot, wrote left-handed, even picked his nose with his left hand. Roger was always well turned out and really stood apart - well, he did from our mob.

Roger had only two drawbacks. One was that he (I'm almost sure) was a United-ite. The other was that he played tennis, which seemed alien behaviour to us, and used to spend hours on the tennis courts in Weston Park under his mother's tuition.

One day, word filtered down to Martin Street that, 'Taylor was playing tennis,' so with the 'Unitedite' factor paramount in our minds, we decided to go up to the Park to give him some non-encouragement.

When Pete, Dennis and I got to the park we all hung on the netting, shouting things like, 'Tha big nelly, Taylor,' 'When tha gonna gerra skirt?' and, 'Is that a blouse tha wearin?'

His mother stopped him from getting at us and tried to keep

his mind on his playing, which would make things worse for him since we'd then start off with, 'Tha freetund of us, Taylor,' and 'Tha'll be playin' chuffin netball next.' We carried on until the park-keeper chased us off.

Later, when we were all in the park playground, Roger turned up. There were two noticeable things about his appearance. Firstly, he was holding a big stick of seaside rock in his hand, (it was the first time I had ever seen seaside rock) and, secondly, he was carrying it in his right hand. The next thing we knew, he'd set about Dennis and me with his left fist. Little Pete slipped into his crying, 'Don't hit me, I'm only little' routine, and got away with it. Roger left us with a warning, 'Keep away from the tennis courts.' Being three public-minded little chaps, we decided we would. Well, who'd want to be responsible for hindering a promising career?

The last time I saw Roger was in 1958 at Owlerton Fun Fair. I was all dressed up in Teddy Boy stuff - velvet collar, drainpipe trousers, that sort of stuff. He was there with his sister. We had a chat, and I said I'd seen reports of him playing tennis in far-off places - Madrid, Budapest and the like. He went on to tell me about the lifestyle of playing in youth tournaments around Europe, how he'd trek all over the place with a sleeping bag and tent on his back, and explained it was not as glamorous as it seemed. So, whatever Roger went on to achieve, I know he worked hard for it.

Years later, I was watching Roger on the television playing at Wimbledon . His opponent was a big Aussie, Bob Hewitt. Old Bob was giving Roger some verbals, and the commentator said, 'I bet there's fun and games in the locker room after this match.' I smiled to myself, thinking, 'I bet I know who will be having the fun.'

Roger went on to play in two Wimbledon semi-finals, which was fantastic considering where he had come from. It was also a tremendous tribute to his mother for all the coaching and time she put in. Whenever I watched him play on TV, I was always cheering inside.

Unfortunately, not all my childhood memories are about heroes, though. I remember I was in my classroom one day, and something happened that upset me very much. At the age I was at the time, I didn't know why it upset me, but it did. We were, all forty odd of us, doing our work, when in came a woman, who, standing and talking in hushed tones to the teacher, pointed at her son, Arnold, who was dressed a mite better than us. (Well, he would be - his mother was wearing a hat and carrying a handbag.) Sitting next to her son was a little kid called Ernest, who was very poorly dressed, even when compared to us ragbags - torn shirt, no trousers' arse, you get the picture. Well, after the chat, the teacher nodded in agreement, and shook the woman's hand. Then, when she'd gone, he started a re-seating shuffle. Arnold ended up sat with someone similarly dressed to him, while Ernest ended up at the front, sat on his own in a two-seater desk. It was clear to us all what had gone on.

When it got to playtime, we all went outside. Arnold sat on a bench, removed his glasses and put them on the seat, so I sat on them and they broke. After playtime, we got back in the classroom and he told the teacher. (Somehow, you just knew he would.) The teacher then asked me if I'd sat on them on purpose. Well, you can guess my answer. No-one in their right mind would answer yes. So Arnold chimes up, 'He did.' It only took the teacher one second to make up his mind who he was going to believe, so he smacked me on the arse with his cane, then led me by the ear to Ernest's desk. I then had to sit by the side of Ern, which was no problem to me. I wasn't dressed much better.

By his actions, the teacher had endorsed the 'us and them' stance, started off by Arnold's mother. The stick and the pulling of my ear didn't hurt me, but little Ern's blushing embarrassment and humiliation did.

At the weekend, sometimes as many as ten of us kids would go together to the Oxford pictures and sit on the front row. One thing we never looked forward to seeing was the news. We found it boring. But there were two characters who would liven things up, if they appeared in the newsreels. They were Churchill and Mahatma Ghandi. If Churchill appeared, the adults would start booing and, although not understanding why, we'd join in, and carry on long after Churchill had left the screen.

On one of my weekly visits to Auntie May's I asked why people booed Churchill, after all, this wasn't long after he'd been our leader and we'd won the war. She explained that during the general strike of the twenties when strikers received no money, an MP from Barnsley stood up pleading for money for food for the strikers' wives and kids who were getting near starvation point. Churchill opposed the motion, saying, 'Let them eat grass,' implying that the working class were nothing but cattle. Then, she told me that a few years later, during the war, he made a rallying call to the working class to fight to the last man. It was alleged at the time that, in the event of Germany occupying Britain, the cabinet, lords and ladies, and the royal family had made provisions to fly off to Canada, so when, in his famous speech, he said, 'We will fight in the streets,' what was meant was, '*You* will fight in the streets.' She added that, after the war, there was a collection in Barnsley to raise money for some sort of lasting tribute to Churchill. 'I think they raised nine pence, and that was nine pence too much.'

On the other hand, when Mahatma Ghandi was on the newsreels, people would cheer. Yet to us he was just a scrawny little bald-headed Indian bloke with glasses, dressed in what looked like a blanket off somebody's bed. Again, Auntie May's opinion was sought. She explained things at my level of understanding, telling me that he united India when Hindus and Muslims were traditionally enemies. She said there were over two million Catholics in India at the time but, eventually, he got his own way with non-violent means. She also told me that all Indians, whatever their religion, hated its lowest cast, 'the untouchables', and would spit on these people, and commit awful atrocities against them. At the height of his popularity, Ghandi went to live with these people to show that he was no better than they were.

Apparently, Ghandi, when he visited London to negotiate independence for India, was offered the choice of hotels. Instead he chose to stay with the working classes of east London. This book is not about politics, but there must be a message in there somewhere for politicians.

One of my earliest memories of my dad was of him with a pot

cast on his leg. He'd taken a job driving a coal lorry and had had an accident. The result was a leg, broken in three places, making it impossible for him to work. In those days, no work meant no money, so he'd applied for 'relief', which was a sort of benefit. Those were hard days. I remember eating a lot of bread and lard, so it couldn't have got much harder. Anyway, this particular day, my dad was nailing down a flattened out biscuit tin lid over a hole in the stairs, when these two blokes dressed in suits walked in without knocking, and one started looking in our cupboards, searching to take stock of what food we had.

'Who the fuckin' 'ell are you?' said dad. One of the blokes replied, 'You have applied for relief, and if we are satisfied, you will have to fill these forms in.' 'Oh, do Ah?' replied my dad. I dived under the table and my mother started crying by the sink. Dad walked past the bloke who was doing the searching, 'Tha 'asn't looked in 'ere,' indicating the sideboard. So he came over to where my dad was standing, near the door. As the bloke bent down to look in the sideboard, my dad grabbed him by the collar and sent him sprawling head first out into the yard. Then, he grabbed the other bloke, who was panicking and saying, 'You will have to fill these forms in,' by the throat. My dad replied, 'They're going ont fuckin' fire,' snatched them out of the man's hand, and chucked them on the few flames which were licking around the couple of pieces of coal which served as fuel for the day. Then, with this bloke still in his grip, he led him, walking backwards, to the open door and shoved him out on his back. The first bloke had done a runner because, by this time, everyone in the yard was out swearing and shouting abuse in support of my dad. The second bloke got up and started running away. While still running he spun round, shouting, 'I'll be back with the police, you have burned the King's property,' meaning the forms. He was then chased off by the neighbours.

During his spell off work, my dad refused help from anyone, although Auntie May used to call and, if he wasn't around, would give my mother home-made bread and buns. Auntie May suddenly started inviting my brother Brian and me around for our tea a couple of times a week. The general feeling of those who lived in our neighbourhood was that we all may have been part of a nation that had won a war, but such as we were still regarded as scum.

A day at Crookesmoor School, in the 1940s, would start off with all the kids congregating in the big hall for assembly. The headteacher would give his address, which centred on a moral message, usually on how to be nice to each other, and we'd sing a few hymns or songs, like 'Onwards Christian Soldiers' and 'Rule Britannia'. The assembly would go on for about half an hour, then we'd troop off to our respective classes, with some virtue or other embedded in our brains.

Our day in the classroom always started off with the register and our teacher would go through the names in alphabetical order - Abbott, Benson and so on. He used to demand you answered with a loud clear, 'Yes, sir.' Then, he'd put a tick or, if you weren't present, a cross. Everyone was scared of the teacher. To show any sort of defiance towards him was regarded as an act of bravery, and your status would shoot up if you ever crossed him. So, one morning, our teacher at the time - I'll call him Mr Cloutem - was going through his usual routine, and getting the required responses. When he got to me, I answered, 'Ah'm 'ere, sir.' Old Cloutem went mad, grabbed his cane - he somehow looked daft without it - dragged me out of my seat, by my ear, to the front of the class, and clouted me on the back of the head. The lights went out for me just for a second. As they were coming back on, I could hear him say, 'Hold your hand out, Pass.' He then smashed the cane down on the palm of my hand, then led me, again by the ear, to my seat, shoved me in it, and carried on with the register as though nothing had happened.

After register, every morning, he'd stand up and beat a rhythm with his stick, and we'd all chant in unison, 'one two is two, two twos are four,' and so on, right through to the twelve times table. All the time, he'd prowl up and down the rows of kids, then, perhaps in the middle of the six times table, he'd smash his stick down on someone's desk, which meant we all had to stop. He'd then point his stick at someone and demand an answer to a question such as, 'Eight fours are?' If they got it wrong, we all had to start again. It seemed like hours sometimes before we got to twelve twelves. Then, when our minds were suitably brainwashed, he'd say something like, 'Now get your history books out, and when you close your desk lids, I don't want to hear a sound.' He used to clout anyone who, for no matter what reason, accidentally or not, made a noise.

Well, one day, after school, seven of us devised a ruse to drive old Mr Cloutem up the wall. After a few hours of practice with bin lids, we had mastered a rhythm of 'knock knock .. na .. knock knock .. knock knock. The next morning, he went through his routine of, 'Close your desks and I don't want to hear a sound,' looked down at his papers, and we swung into action. We'd got it absolutely perfect and, as the noises came from all different parts of the classroom, he hadn't a clue who was responsible. He went up the wall and demanded that the culprits own up.

'No work will be done until they do,' he declared, and you could almost read all the class's minds. A sort of 'that'll do for us', so we sat in stone-cold silence while he tapped his own hand with the cane, obviously dying to get swinging with it. It was so silent that you could hear the birds singing outside, and in the distance some class or other belting out 'All things bright and beautiful'. Eventually, Cloutem decided to do a bit of detective work. He wrote on the blackboard the number of knocks required to produce our little ditty.

He came to the conclusion that it was seven, and as he knew that the noises came from different parts of the classroom, he had seven subjects to find. He seemed visibly pleased. Obviously, dying to use that stick. Still no volunteers, so he declared he was going to pick seven kids at random. He started off by picking Raggy Ernest, and I thought, 'The bastard, he'll not pick Mrs Chuffin' Handbag's lad.' So, there was old Ern, looking a bit pathetic at the front of the class and crying his eyes out. Then someone shouted out, 'It weren't 'im, it wo me.' I wish I could say that I was the one who shouted out, but I can't. Cloutem gave this little kid four strokes of the cane, and said he was going to carry on until he shopped the rest of us. He promptly told on us and we all got caned.

Not long after this incident, Mr Cloutem was off sick (probably with tennis elbow or something to do with exertion with the stick), and we got a relief teacher. On his first day, he sat at his desk and placed his lunchbox on his table. On top of his lunchbox he placed an apple and an orange. Then, he started his register. I'd been dared by the others to answer, 'Ah'm 'ere sir,' so, of course, I did. He hesitated, looked up, then carried on.

At the end of the register reading, he called out, 'Will Fred Pass come to the front, please?' As I walked to the front I was thinking, 'I'm in it now. I hope he hasn't got a club or a machine gun or anything.' 'I noticed that you answered differently to all the other children. Do you answer your regular teacher 'yes, sir' when reading the register?' he asked. I nodded in acknowledgement. 'Well, I admire individuality, and you should be suitably rewarded.' As I was thinking, 'Oh, ah,' he went on, 'Hold out your hand.' By this time, I was thinking, 'Ah've been 'ere before.' He then placed his apple in my hand, and said to the class, 'Will you all stand please, and join me in applauding Fred,' at which everyone, including the teacher, started clapping while my face was going through all the colours in the warm end of the spectrum. The clapping went on for ages. He then signalled them to stop, saying, 'Let's round it off with three cheers,' and added, 'Why not?' Meanwhile, I had only one thought. 'Why didn't I keep my bleedin' mouth shut?'

When I'd finally sat down, he said, 'In the morning, please answer my register call in any way you see fit, there will be no inhibitions in this class.' The next morning everyone, including me, answered with a 'yes, sir.'

We couldn't believe it. We had to find out what would make him mad. So we decided to try him out with our knock knock .. na ..

knock knock routine. We did and he responded by saying, 'Hey, that was good, who did it?' I could already see more apples coming my way. Anyway, in a matter of seconds we all owned up, and he asked us how we did it, declaring, 'That's great choreography, could you do it quieter for me?' … and so on. So, we spent about fifteen minutes showing off our little prank, after which he said, 'Thank you very much lads, you will be rewarded.'

A couple of days later the teacher turned up with a football, and announced that we were going to have football practice as our PE lesson. We all smacked our lips at the prospect. He then added, 'Except our Busby Berkley seven. As a reward, I've arranged with the music teacher (we called her Miss Flabbergasted, because that's how she always looked) for you to have extra tuition in music, because you've really got something there, lads.'

I'll leave you to make up your mind who was the best teacher. Perhaps people who call for the cane to be brought back should really be thinking along other lines, for the teacher who didn't hit us commanded utter respect, the other none. With one teacher you could look forward to going to school, with the other you'd try anything to avoid going. With one teacher you'd listen to every word. With the other you'd be determined not to take notice, thinking, 'If he thinks that's right - well it must be wrong.'

Chapter 11

Bad Times

Sometimes, I'd get home from school and the alternative to what mother was doing for tea was bread and dripping or bread and treacle. If the main offering was tripe, chittling and bag, cow heel, or - worst of all - pig's trotters, I'd always plump for the dripping. Needless to say, there was no need for slimming clubs in the forties.

One day, I arrived home from school and my mother was sitting looking up at the ceiling, moaning, 'I want to die, I want to die.' On her lap was an empty opened purse. 'Mam, it's me, Fred,' I said as I tugged at her arm. She seemed oblivious to me, so I got a cup and pushed a chair up against the sink, climbed up, and put some water in the cup from out of the tap. I didn't know what good it would do, but it was the only thing I could think of.

'Here, Mam, have a drink,' I said, pressing the cup into her hand. She still went on repeating, 'I want to die.' By this time, my heart and stomach were welling up inside, and I could feel my pulse pounding in my head as I tried to pull her up out of the chair, crying my eyes out all the time. I dashed across the yard to Mrs Aistrop's. 'Me mam wants to die,' I blurted out. Mrs Aistrop dashed passed me and into our house to have a look at my mother. 'Goo and get thi dad,' was all she said.

My dad was working at the Hallamshire on 'afternoons' at the time. On Fridays, when it was payday, my mother would meet him and he'd give her the housekeeping money so she could do the shopping. I think they call it 'living from hand to mouth'. It was 1948, and I was six years old, and for other, later-to-be-explained reasons, the year would be a bad one for me.

From Martin Street to the Hallamshire was perhaps about a mile which, for me with my little legs, seemed a very long way. With Mrs Aistrop's words, '… and be as quick as you can,' ringing in my ears, I was off, running and crying at the same time. When I got to the Hallamshire, I entered a big gateway into what seemed like a big black aeroplane hanger. I left the brightness of day behind, still crying about the state my mother was in. Then, I had another reason to cry - fear at entering this big black hole of a place, which produced deafening sounds and was full of black smoke. All I could see were red-hot bars zooming around like big red snakes. The floor was covered in steel plates and, as I tentatively walked forward, I was sure I was going to drop down some big hole.

All of a sudden, a bloke walked towards me out of the blackness. 'Come on young un, tha can't come in 'ere.' I just wailed, 'Weerz me dad?' still crying. 'Who's ya dad?' 'Fred Pass.' The bloke shouted into the darkness, 'Oy Fred, your young un's ere.' My dad appeared from out of the blackness. 'What the bleedin' 'ell's tha doin ere?' 'It's mam. She says she wants to die.' At this he scooped me up under his arm, and off we dashed towards Martin Street.

While my dad ran with me under his arm, it felt as though my rib cage was being crushed in, nevertheless, I found the pain reassuring. Strangely, it made me feel better about the situation, so it never crossed my mind to complain. I just wanted to get home, all the time thinking, 'I hope my mam's still alive.'

By the time we got back, the house was full of neighbours. My dad put me down in the yard, with the instructions to stay there, while he entered the house. Some kids were playing football in our yard, and one of them shouted, 'Does tha want a game, Fred.' It fell on deaf ears, probably for the first time in my life, as I paced around, not able to take my eyes off our doorway. Then my Dad shouted me in. I dashed to my mother. 'Aya orl reight, mam?' 'Come 'ere,' she said and cuddled me on her knee. I breathed a huge sigh of relief as she whispered in my ear, 'Everything's gonna be alright.'

Years later, when I was a grown man, I often asked my mother the reason for her distress that day. The only answer I ever got was, 'I can't remember,' so I'll never know.

Thinking of my mother's anguish at the time, I've come to the conclusion that, back in the forties, the husband worked and the wife took on - well - everything else. My mother became a buffer against whatever life could throw and, back then, there certainly was some stuff flying about. She didn't even tell him when I got into trouble (which was, occasionally, known to happen). She'd threaten to tell him but, to my knowledge, she never did. I suppose my mother's distressed state that day arose from life's constant buffeting.

At the age of about five, I started to have involuntary movements of my body - sort of nervous twitches of arms, legs, and neck. I also found out that, when I sat down, I couldn't keep still. My knees would tremble, not constantly, but erratically, so my mother took me to Doctor Rigby's. Consequently, every morning before going to school, I had the radio doctor, the shipping forecaster, and a tablespoon of cod liver oil. What a way to start the day. I didn't know it at the time, but I had an illness which was to turn out to be, in layman terms, St Vitus' Dance.

I vividly remember going with my mother, one day, to Meadow Street for my hair cutting. I sat in the barber's chair, while she gave him his instructions - short back and sides and a lot off the top. (Well, you had to get maximum value for your money in those days.) She also gave me *my* instructions. 'Keep still or you'll get the scissors stuck in your head.' Well, being suitably motivated, I made a concentrated effort not to move. The result was an awful sensation, which seemed to swell up from my stomach to my brain, coupled with a sickly feeling. I felt I was slipping away, with everything in sight slowly getting dimmer and dimmer, as though I had a dimmer switch in my head. There was a bang - and then blackness.

As I came round, it felt like someone was turning the dimmer switch up, and everything came back into focus. The drawback was that, after the blackout, I wanted to throw up, and it took so much out of me that I couldn't stand. My mother left me in the barber's while she went off to borrow a pushchair in order to get me home. This was my first encounter with 'Mr Blackout', and I was to have many more. To rectify the problem, I was sent to see a specialist at the Children's Hospital. As we entered his room, I swear that, by holding my mother's hand, I could feel her apprehension travel through to me.

After the examination the specialist told me curtly to get dressed. One of the things that I couldn't do was button up my shirt.

My mother began to help me, but the man interrupted her, saying, 'Let him do it himself.' I don't know if he said this to judge the extent of my illness but, what with him looking on with a miserable expression on his face, and with my mother's face full of apprehension, I started to cry as my hands tried in vain to put the buttons though the button holes. The specialist finally uttered two words. 'Help him,' he sneered, and left the room in what looked like disgust to me.

I became a regular visitor at the Children's Hospital. I went, one day, to find that (we'll call him Dr Goebels because I can't remember his real name) Dr Goebels had been replaced by a lady doctor, a certain Doctor Gordon who, in contrast to old Goebels, was like a breath of fresh air.

She'd bend down and look me in the eyes and say, 'Hello Freddie, and what have you been up to?' I'd look down at my shoes and reply, 'Nowt,' then blush at such open friendliness. After my examination she'd say, 'Now, let's have a look at these pesky buttons,' and help me dress. She'd end my visit by ruffling my hair and saying, 'Let me see if I have something for you,' before producing a sweet. I'd leave the hospital smiling.

It's nearly sixty years since I last saw Doctor Gordon, but I'll never forget her. As for the other doctor, I'm reduced to making up scathing nicknames for him.

Then came the day I would never forget. The previous night, Auntie May had visited our house saying, 'You can borrow this,' giving my mother a tiny suitcase. All evening they spoke in hushed tones and, if it became obvious I was trying to listen, would shut up.

The next morning, my mother got me ready and we set off, she carrying the little suitcase.

'Where are we goin'.'
'To see someone in Macclesfield.'
'Where's Macclesfield?'

She just mumbled something. I was getting suspicious. If anything good was ever on the horizon - Christmas, birthdays, or anything like that, as a kid, you'd always get a week's notice, so that you could look forward to it. So, in this situation, the silence was deafening.

We changed buses somewhere or other. When we finally got off the bus at Macclesfield, there was this man waiting in a car. He greeted my mother and we got into the back. It was the very first time I 'd ever travelled in a car and, while I didn't understand why, the situation felt definitely sinister. The car drove up this gravely path, which led to a big detached, posh-looking house, alien to anything I'd ever seen before. In front of the house was a large manicured lawn with canvas camp beds dotted about, some containing kids who were sleeping. A woman, who seemed pleasant enough, led me to one of these camp beds. 'You have a little sleep, Freddie, while I have a chat with your mum.'

I was now really suspicious. I'd travelled all this way, a bloke in a car was waiting for us, and a woman who I'd never seen before was calling me by my first name. 'How did she know my name?' I was thinking, as I lay in the camp bed.

I was awoken by the woman calling, 'Come along children, time for tea.' I thought she was referring to all the other kids and not me, for I had come with 'me mam' and that's the way I was going back. So, while all the other kids went rushing towards the house, I stood my ground. The woman offered out the back of her hand to me. 'Come along for some tea, Freddie.' 'Weerz me mam?' I asked. 'I want me mam.' Then, with a few words, she cut me adrift from all my emotions. 'Your mum's gone home. You'll be staying with us for a while.'

It felt as though my stomach was going to drop through my arse. All of a sudden my bottom lip seemed uncontrollable and I was lost in space, unable to comprehend what was happening. Why had my mother gone off? No goodbyes. I'd been left, and it felt like it. When you see present-day space travellers doing their space walks attached to the mother ship by a lifeline, well, that was me and my lifeline had been cut.

As the woman led me towards the house, my mind was working overtime. I was desperate to find a conclusion which would explain my predicament. Suddenly, putting two and two together, I came up with the customary five. 'Oh no! **The Homes.** I'm in a home for bad kids.' My mother had often warned me about them, and said that's where I'd end up.

I could act a bit, to get my own way, so I started pleading dramatically, 'Let me go home to me mam, Ah'll be a good lad'. I kept repeating, 'Ah'll be a good lad,' crying and sobbing all the time. Suddenly, I realised I wasn't acting.

The woman was nice enough. 'Don't cry Freddie, you'll like it

77

here.' She led me into the house, and paraded me in front of about a dozen or so smartly dressed kids, all about my age. 'This is Freddie, he's going to be with us for a while so, in turn, will you all tell him your name.' Each kid said his first name, and I stood there in total emotional shock. Every one spoke in a different accent. This, in itself, seemed sinister to me.

Then, one lad said his name was Dennis. That was it Dennis was my pal's name in Martin Street - so I turned round, and quick as a flash, ran down the gravely path, heading off home. The next thing I knew, the bloke of the house caught up with me, slapped my arse and warned, 'Don't ever do that again.' He took me back into the house. It was the first time I'd ever been hit in my life.

That first night was horrendous. I just couldn't stop crying and wondering what my mam and dad were doing a million miles away in Martin Street. I was sleeping in a large bedroom with about four or five other kids. We were all in single beds and, what with the crying and fidgeting around I was doing, I was making a terrible racket. In came the bloke again, he slapped my arse once more and then led me to a passageway to a camp bed by a window. He drew the curtains. 'That's where you'll sleep until you learn to behave yourself.'

I lay there in total blackness, and in something much worse - total despair. I felt as though I'd been given a life sentence and no release date. So, within twenty-four hours I, at the age of six, had become an orphan, a prisoner, friendless, and a castaway.

Over the next few weeks, I gradually began to settle, and got into the routine. The woman of the house sort of took me under her wing so, if we ever went out in a group, she'd hold my hand. I often used to ask if my mother was coming, and she'd answer, 'Soon Freddie, soon.' I never believed her, and never thought I'd ever go home.

The daily routine was that you'd get up in a morning, wash yourself, go downstairs, and all sit around the table. The bloke would sit at one end, and the woman at the other end. He'd say, 'And now we'll say grace.' The first time he said it, I thought, 'Who's chuffin' grace?' Anyway, every kid used to say the usual 'for what we are about to receive' bit, and the bloke would say, 'You can begin to start eating.' The food was very good. Breakfast would start off with porridge, then bacon and eggs, toast and marmalade and cups of tea - in cups - with saucers!

Everything was going fine, until one morning when I was washing my plate and cup and saucer (it was part of the deal to wash up after yourself) and the woman was singing to herself. Then, she switched on the radio and I just heard the back end of the weather forecast, and caught the word 'Dogger.' My entire mind was instantly flush with memories of Martin Street and tears ran down my cheeks.

As the weeks went on, the woman patiently explained that I wasn't there as a punishment, but to help me get better. The couple looking after us would organise sports days, egg and spoon races, sack races and the like. The woman would take us on nature walks and explain all sorts of things to us. At first, I was scared of the noise the trees made when it got windy, but I saw an owl, a fox and a badger, and generally began to enjoy it. It must have been autumn while I was there because all the leaves were coming off the trees. We'd all collect some and, when we got back, we'd stick them in scrapbooks. I remember they had a goat who was chained up and, if he didn't know you, I was warned, he'd try to butt you. In the end I'd been there that long, I'd reached the stage when I could stroke 'Old Billy' and he didn't mind at all.

One afternoon, when I'd finished sticking my leaves into the scrapbook, I asked the woman if I could feed Old Billy some old bread crusts. 'Yes Freddie, and can you guess who's coming to see you on Saturday? Your dad and mum!' It must have been two months or more since I'd last seen them and the shock seemed almost as bad as when I'd been left there in the first place.

I don't know why I wasn't glad to hear the news, but my emotions were in turmoil. Although the news was good, I felt bad in myself. The only way to describe it would be for you to imagine throwing all your emotions into a tumble dryer for a couple of weeks, then stop the machine, and, after a couple of months, turning it back on again.

When my dad and mam came on the Saturday, I couldn't hold myself back. I ran to my dad, he scooped me up, and told the woman that they were going to take me into Macclesfield for the afternoon. I had my haircut - and didn't have a blackout. My dad bought me an ice cream. He also bought me a toy Indian and bison, then told me I was coming home the following week. The week after, I was transferred to the Children's Hospital in Sheffield, stayed overnight, and next day after a series of tests, was back in Martin Street via an ambulance.

At tea-time, we all sat down at the table. 'Who's saying grace?' I asked. My dad looked aghast. 'What thi bleedin' done to thee?' Trying to tone it down, I then asked, 'Can we start, dad?' 'Chuffin' 'ell,' he breathed.

I've since made enquiries about the convalescent home and my time there, and the only things I found out was that I was admitted on 22 June 1948, and the name of the place was 'Swansea House'. I also discovered that, in all probability, the blackouts I'd been suffering from were epileptic fits - something I was lucky to grow out of.

Chapter 12

A Day at the Seaside

The highlight of our year on Martin Street, and surrounding areas, was the annual club trip to the seaside. The local working men's clubs - in our case, Radford Street Club, later to be known as St Phillips Road Club - would provide a free day out for all the local kids. You also got spending money, plus a dinner of fish and chips.

The money for these trips was raised through weekly raffles. Each man who was a member of the club would receive two tickets for the trip. Somehow, even if your dad wasn't a member, you'd still end up with a ticket.

I went on my first club trip when I was about seven. My mother took me up to the club at around seven o'clock one Sunday morning. All my pals were there and, by the time the charabancs arrived, there must have been three hundred kids queuing. Dennis, Lawrence, Pete and I stuck together, so we'd all get on the same chara.

A bloke walked up and down the queue shouting, 'If ya want to gu tut lav gu nah, cuz wi not stoppin'.' The result was three hundred kids pissing all over the place.

Anyone under eight years old had a cardboard label attached to his or her coat lapel with a bit of string. On the label was your name and address, just in case you got lost. The older lads used to poke fun at these labels so, as soon as the bloke who'd attached the label wasn't looking, you took it off.

We all piled on the coach, full of excitement at the prospect of a whole day in Cleethorpes. We sat laughing and chattering in excited anticipation. The driver got on plus Bert, a bloke whose job it was to supervise and be of help, should any problems arise. Bert was armed with two crates of brown ale. He slammed the chara's door and shouted, 'Right, we're off.' All the little kids waved through the window at their mothers as the chara pulled away.

Bert announced his code of conduct, once he had the silence that he'd demanded. 'Anybody messin' abaht gets chucked off an', as Ah teld ya befoor, wi not stoppin'.' Bert then opened a bottle of beer and gave it to the driver, before opening one for himself. About half an hour into the journey, Little Pete observed, 'Iz a good driver, 'e can drive wi one 'and. Bet wiv got best un.'

Halfway through the journey, Bert came down the chara with a shoe-box full of wage packets, each containing two half crowns, five bob in all. He passed them out to the kids saying, 'Don't loyse it.' He was continually interrupted by a loud belch or fart, to which he declared 'good arse'.

When we got to Cleethorpes, we all joined in singing 'for he's a jolly good driver'. We could vouch for that, because he'd driven a lot of the way, indeed nearly all the way, with a bottle of beer in his hand. The coaches pulled up by the station approach, opposite the fish and chip restaurant where we were to have our dinner. Bert's final instructions were, again, what you could call 'basic'. 'Queue artside 'ere for ya dinner,' pointing across to the fish place, 'and be back 'ere fo' six toneet.' The last thing he said made my hair stand on end, 'and anybody late, wi leervin ya.'

The fish and chip place was a big imposing three-storey building. It had to be to accommodate three hundred kids. The scene inside was total bedlam. Kids flicking peas at each other, flying chips, an odd skimming slice of bread and butter. Each waitress was dressed in the customary black dress, white pinny, and a white cotton thing, which looked like a tiara, gripped to her hair.

We were on the top floor, so they had to cart all the fish and chips up two lots of stairs. The noise was deafening and, what with all the missiles flying about, the waitresses really looked hampered on their way to the tables, carrying about four plates of fish and chips each. Someone pulled an apron undone from behind, causing it to drop on the floor. The waitress put the fish and chips down and, when she bent down to pick up the apron, some kid gave her tiara-like headdress a tug, leaving it cocked over on one side. The sight of that waitress with a blood red face, headdress on one side, having the occasional slip on a chip, dodging flying peas, was one I will never forget. I suppose Sigmund Freud, if he'd surveyed the scene in the fish place, would have concluded that it was a reaction brought about by the repressive authoritarian and social structure of the times. In fact, it was pure anarchy for anarchy's sake.

The meal out of the way, we were off to explore the delights of Cleethorpes. On getting to the front, someone said, 'Oh, look at sea.' Dennis calmly countered, 'It's Humber.' Jenks looked at him. 'Tha what?' 'It's the River Humber,' Dennis repeated, 'Ah've looked it up at school.' 'What tha talking abaht, that's not a chuffin river,'

Jenks said, pointing to this vast amount of water, 'Tha'd be oreight tryin' to catch sticklebacks in that lot.' The 'that lot' triggered me off, remembering the countless 'what lot, this lot, that lot' conversations I'd had with my mam, so I said, 'Shurrup bleedin' arguing 'n come on.'

On our walk around the shops in Cleethorpes, we called in a gift shop to buy a penny peashooter each, as we all had a pocketful of uneaten peas from the fish place. They were like little green ball bearings. The chef probably thought, 'Three hundred kids from Sheffield. Chuff 'em.'

Anyway, I was standing at the counter to one side, and there was this couple before us, and the man asked the price of a beach ball which was hanging up. The woman behind the counter told him that it was one and sixpence, and the bloke started scratching his chin. While he was mulling over the investment, the woman behind the counter shouted into the back of the shop, 'Bill, have we any more of these beach balls in the back?' My eyes switched to 'Bill' through a door which was ajar. I could see him there, near a great big net full of these very same beach balls. Bill replied, 'No love, that's the very last.' So the bloke who'd been contemplating buying the ball promptly said, 'Ah'll tek it.' I suppose I was witnessing a lesson in salesmanship.

The day went as planned, or as unplanned, as it could be. We'd almost spent up within a couple of hours, but had each saved a tanner to buy something to take back as a present for our mothers (we were good lads, see), so we were wondering around 'Wonderland' amusement arcade with no disposable cash.

Incidentally, the name of the place was self-descriptive. Inside, there were all sorts of fairground-type rides around the edge of the building, which was like a big hangar. There were side attractions - the house of mirrors, the haunted house, that sort of thing. It didn't take Dennis long to notice that each of these places had an 'in' sign and an 'out' sign, and that there was always someone sat in a small cubicle at the 'in' sign, but no-one at the 'out' sign. 'So what?' sneered Jenks. Dennis explained that we could all go in the 'out' entrance, have a look around, then come back out the 'out' entrance at no cost. It worked a treat and, as they used to say, 'A good time was had by one and all.'

Years later, when my family and I visited Stratford on Avon, I told my kids of this merry jape. We came across William Shakespeare's birthplace, so to prove my point to the kids, I went in the 'out' door, had a look round, and came back out the 'out' door. The kids thought it funny. Sandra, my wife, said that I was like a big kid. I suppose I can't argue with that.

Back in Cleethorpes, we got down to the serious business of trying to find something to buy for our mams as presents. We finally plumped for having a go on the elephant machine. You had to put your tanner in and, out of a hole in a cave scene, came this little toy elephant on what looked like a small railway track. The track was semi-circular. When the elephant got to the front of the tableau, a table on its back tipped off a small white cardboard box and it went down a chute. You retrieved your box from the bottom of the machine and looked at what you'd got. This time, Pete got a little plastic ring. Dennis and Jenks got the same - a tiny 'present from

Cleethorpes' sugar spoon - and I got a tie-pin. I comforted myself by thinking, 'Still, Ah can gi it mi dad for Christmas.'

Pete did his crying routine after slipping the ring into his pocket. The bloke who ran the arcade came to see what the fuss was about, and Pete showed him the empty box. We all stood around watching with quivering bottom lips. We weren't pretending, Pete was that good! It didn't take long before the bloke produced a big bunch of keys, unlocked the back of the machine, and gave Pete another box. It was a tie-pin, so Pete was happy. He'd got a ring for his mother and a tie-pin for his dad.

Anyway, we all trudged back to the chara, feeling good. We'd had a good day. Back on board, Bert, complete with another crate of brown ale, did a quick count, interrupting with a few 'keep chuffin' stills' and a couple of 'good arses', then declared, 'Right, we're off.' Halfway back, Bert lurched down the coach handing out bags of crisps, plain with a little blue bag of salt in them. Smith's crisps. These were the only kind that existed. Also an orange each, and a little bottle of pop. After distributing all these goodies, Bert called for everyone's attention by saying, 'Bleedin' shurrup a bit.' He then offered some delicate advice regarding the pop. 'Don't sup pop till ya nearly ooam or yule be pissin' orl o'er.' We liked old Bert. He and the driver didn't bother us and let us enjoy ourselves.

When we'd had our pops and were getting a bit bored, we decided to use our peashooters. The targets were Bert and the driver. The driver was the first target because he had a bald head, which made him very inviting, if you happened to have a peashooter in your hand. Jenks had the first bull's-eye - right on the bald head.

The pea hit, and bounced off. No reaction. So, we switched our attentions to Bert. He was wearing a cap, so his neck was the target. Whoosh! Spot on, but still no reaction. After this had gone on for a while, we decided on another plan of action - a sort of a four-gun volley at the driver's bald head. Jenks counted down, 'One, two, three, **fire**.' We fired off four shots, spot on - thud, thud, thud, thud. No reaction. At this point, we just gave the game up. The only conclusion I can come to is that the driver must have been comatose due to the brown ale.

As we saw St Phillip's Club in the distance, we sang, 'For he's a jolly good driver and so say all of us.' Well, we'd been safely driven there, one-handed, and driven back the same way, despite him having the early signs of rigor mortis.

As we all trooped off the coach, one of the waiting parents shouted, 'Ave thi been good, Bert?' 'As good as gold,' Bert replied, adding, 'No trouble at all.'

We all got out of the coach, leaving a carpet of orange peel, crisps, crisp bags, about fifty empty bottles rolling about and two or three little streams, which were just reaching the front. Well, he had said we weren't stopping.

Back home, my dad was the first to quiz me about the day's events.

"Ave ya 'ad a good day, Fred lad?'
'Smashin'.'
'Who were in charge of your chara?'
'Bert.'

"Aye, iz good wi kids, Bert.'

I often think back to those trips and laugh, but years later I have nothing but respect for the working men's clubs in and around Sheffield, because they provided a free day out to thousands of kids who wouldn't normally have ever had the chance to visit the seaside. It was an example of the working class looking after its own. There were no government-funded free days out. The government at the time probably thought it better to spend money on borstals. As for old Bert, there were many like him. I'm sure he could have found better things to do than accompany fifty screaming kids to Cleethorpes. The trips, the Berts, the working men's clubs, to me mean human nature at its best.

Chapter 13

The Visit

One day, our teacher announced that the following week we were having a visitor from the education authority. He said he'd be acting in the capacity of an observer for the day. 'So while he's here,' the teacher said, 'and before I read the register, I will address you by saying, "Good morning, children," (I thought, 'Chuffin' 'ell iz never done that before.') and you will reply, "Good morning, Sir," and, as usual, when I read the register, you will reply, "Here, Sir," and nothing else.'

He paused at this point, looked straight at me, and said, 'Are you listening, Pass?' I nodded to acknowledge him. He repeated, 'Are you listening, Pass?' only this time a little louder and more slowly. I replied, 'Yes.' The teacher then said, 'Yes, what?' So I replied, 'Yes, I'm listening.' By now he was getting agitated and bawled out, 'Yes, I'm listening, what?' with the emphasis on 'what'. So I said, 'Yes, I'm listening a lot.' At this, he grabbed his cane and marched up to my desk, gave it a great whack, and said, 'Yes, I'm listening a lot, what?' It sounded so daft that all the class broke out in giggles. I was being mischievous and wanted to torment him to the limit, but even *I* was becoming concerned that he was in danger of slipping over the edge. I was glad he'd only got a cane and not a gun.

He grabbed me by the ear and marched me to the front of the class. 'Now, Pass,' he said, pausing briefly to shout at the class,

'Stop that laughing, or I'll cane the lot of you. Now, Pass, I said, "Are you listening?"' By now I was scared and also didn't want his question to turn into a rival to War and Peace, so I said, 'Yes, Sir.' 'Oh! You have finally remembered your manners, have you? So just don't forget them, especially next week. I'm going to give you two strokes. They may help the lesson sink in.' *Whack, whack.* 'Sit down!'

When we arrived at school the next Monday morning, our visitor was sitting at the front of the class, on one side of the teacher. One looked so much like the other that they could have been brothers. The visitor was wearing a three-piece pin-stripped suit, stiff collared shirt and a totally humourless expression. I reflected, 'I bet he's dished some stick out in his time.' If you've ever seen a film where uniformed Germans were torturing a prisoner, inevitably the door of the cell would swing open and in would walk some cultured well-dressed bloke, straight away you'd think 'sinister'. Well, that describes our visitor to a tee, even though he looked a bit daft with his notebook and pen, sitting behind a desk that was designed for ten year olds.

We settled down and were all sitting at our desks with our teacher standing in front of us. He looked out of place somehow. Something wasn't quite right. Then it came to me. His cane. There was no sign of the cane. I thought, 'How's he going to cope without a cane?' He looked like a drummer sat at the drums with no stick.

The other unusual thing was that our teacher was smiling - and that didn't look right at all. With people who aren't used to smiling, when they do, they have a sort of wild-eyed satanic look about then. Have you noticed?

Anyway, he kicked off the day with his specially choreographed 'Good morning, children' and said it with a big wild-eyed smile. Everyone except me replied, 'Good morning, Sir.' I said, 'Good morning, shitbag,' which couldn't be heard by anyone else but my desk-mate, Ronnie Grainger. My reply had been drowned in the unison of everybody's 'Good morning, Sir.' On hearing my reply, Ronnie burst out laughing. That was normally good for a couple of strokes and, with it happening so early, would have set the scene for the rest of the day. So, what was our teacher's reaction, bearing in mind Dr Death was watching from behind his little desk? 'Oh, Ronald,' he said, 'I can see you are in a cheerful mood today. That's what I like to see, cheerful children,' while I thought, 'You like to see happy children about as much as a mouse likes to see a mousetrap.'

The teacher went through his register routine without any hiccups and looked visibly relieved when the chore was completed. The only difference I noticed was that, when he got to my name, he pronounced it 'Parse' not 'Pass'. I was about to question his pronunciation, but then thought better of it.

Everyday, we'd start with maths, which consisted of repeating your times tables in unison, starting at two times and finishing at twelve. But not this day. Before starting the work, he'd normally demand that someone, 'Open the windows and let God's air in.' It was normally me, most times, who had to get a big pole about six feet in length with a brass hook on the end of it to pull down the catch on the windows and open them up. I was always scared that I'd put the pole through a window. Anyway, this particular morning, he opened the window himself (the first and, no doubt, the last time). Eventually, he started the day with ,'Right, children,' (He'd never called us that before, either) 'our first lesson of the day is English and, as usual, I will try to make it interesting.' 'Interesting?!' His usual English lessons consisted of clouting kids for spelling mistakes and, as I couldn't spell, I was always the chief recipient. (To this day, I still can't spell, which is probably due to him.)

The teacher then pointed to a kid called Norman and asked, 'What are your favourite kinds of films, Norman?' Norman was a bit dumbstruck by this, but eventually replied, 'Cowboys.' The teacher knew he was on safe ground with his question to Norm because, a couple of days before, he'd caned him for bringing his cowboy's gun to school. He'd belittled Norm at the time. So, having had Norman's answer, the teacher wrote 'cowboys' in chalk on the blackboard and underlined it.

'Now, children, the lesson will test your observational powers, so I will be asking you for associated words connected to our subject of cowboys.' Straight away, I shot my hand up, but he ignored me and was about to go rabbiting on, when old Doctor Death gave a nervous little cough to indicate my raised arm to the teacher. 'Yes, Freddie?' the teacher enquired (Freddie was another 'just for today' expression.) 'What do you mean, Sir?' He looked relieved that my question didn't embarrass him in any way, in fact, he seemed to like it so much he was off in a flurry of words, 'Well, Freddie, I want people to come up here and under my heading of 'cowboys' write something to do with cowboys, that way it will demonstrate that a visit to the pictures can, in some small way, prove to be educational.' I thought this was all turning really sickly and, deep down, I preferred his other personality to this one. I wondered what he was going to do next.

'Terrence, will you start us off, please?' His question was asked in a sort of off-the-cuff way. He knew he was on safe ground with Terry, who was bit brighter than the rest of us and a true conformist. Terry walked up and wrote 'hat'. 'Very good,' said the teacher, then threw it open to the class by inviting, 'Anyone else?' All the hands shot up, including mine. One by one, the kids went up to the blackboard and wrote things such as 'spurs', 'chaps', 'waistcoat' and so on.

The teacher had been deliberately ignoring my up-raised hand, but was fast running out of volunteers. In the end, he had no option, so I walked up to the blackboard, intending to write the word 'pistol'. After writing the first three letters, I deliberately dropped the chalk. As I bent down to look for it, I gave the class a good view of my first three letters. 'Come on, Freddie, where's the chalk?' the teacher said. 'Ah can't find it, Sir', I replied. One or two in the class were giggling and the teacher was getting flustered. In desperation he hissed, 'Never mind, have a new stick of chalk.' His intense stare said, 'You're in it, lad.'

I held the new chalk with two fingers at the very base so, as soon as I put any pressure on it, the chalk broke. The whole class was now laughing at my uncompleted word. I bent down to look for the broken bit and the teacher barked, 'Never mind, just complete your word - and quiet please, children.' The drummer was definitely struggling without his sticks. I finally sat down and everyone received a 'well done', except me. I looked across to see that old Doctor Death was wearing a 'we have ways of making you talk' expression on his face. Once back in my seat, Ronnie said the obvious: 'Daz 'ad it fo' dat.'

Sure enough, the next day, I sat next to Ronnie and said, conversationally, 'Cowd this morning init?' 'That's it,' said the teacher. 'Out here, Pass.' (He'd dropped the Freddie bit.) The drummer had got his sticks back and warmed up by giving me a couple of strokes. *Whack, whack.* 'Sit down!' And the day began with. 'One two is two, two twos are four.... ' Monday morning, and the rest of the week, were in full swing.

Fred (aged 2) with his brother, Brian (aged 9), 1944.

*Fred (aged 6) and his mother
1948 on the miniature railway at Cleethorpes.*

*Fred as a baby with his mother's family.
Fred's grandfather is seated, centre.*

Fred (aged 8) with Aunty May and cousin Marlene Blackpool 1950.

Fred (aged 9) Blackpool 1951.

Fred's dad (1913-1976) drawn by Fred himself.

Chapter 14

Iz 'ere

'Weerz me dad?' was probably my most-used phrase when I was small. I never seemed to see much of him. My question was usually answered with, 'at work'. My dad spent about thirty years, in all, working at the Hallamshire Steel and File Rolling Mills on Neepsend Lane. He spent most of those years as bottom man in a team of about ten people. He worked three shifts - mornings: 6am to 2pm, afternoons: 2pm to 10pm and nights: 10pm to 6am. This was done on alternate weeks and, what with his sleeping after work, I just never seemed to see him, not as much as I wanted to anyway. He was a bad-tempered, abrasive, blunt, uneducated, caring, warm, gentle, honest, independent bloke.

One of my earliest memories of him recalls a night when I was in bed in Martin Street. It was the middle of the night and I was on my stomach peering out of our bedroom window holding my chin up with the palms of my hand. I saw two blokes, carrying two massive sacks, coming down our entry. My dad was in the next bed to me. I pulled at his arm. 'Dad, dad look!' He turned over, had a look, then said, 'Get to sleep.' I still continued, 'But dad ...' He repeated his order, but in stronger terms, 'Ah sed get to sleep!'

The next day, one of these blokes came to our house with half a dozen pairs of brand new shoes. He didn't knock, no one ever did, except for collectors and their kind. My dad was reading the paper and this bloke announced, 'Ah've brought ya summat, Fred,' offering my dad the shoes. 'Ah don't want owt forrum, thi thine.' My dad's answer was not ambiguous. 'Tek thi shoes an' fuck off.' The bloke went on. 'Tek um, Fred. Nobdy 'no's thi missin'.' Then my dad started getting angry. My mother never said a word. She just looked uncomfortable. I was starting to get scared. 'Ah 'no', that's good enough for me and Ah sharn't tell thi agee'rn.' The bloke jumped in in a bit of a panic, 'Don't …' My dad cut him short with, 'If tha mutters, "Don't sey owt", Ah'll chuck thi through that fuckin' door, so tek thi shoes, an' fuck off!'

Once the bloke had gone, there was a short uneasy silence. Dad then muttered, 'Yu've seen nowt, yu've 'eared nowt, an' ya sey nowt.' He said it in such a way that it stuck. He then carried on reading his paper. Next day, on the way to school, it sounded like a load of mice were on Martin Street. All the kids from our area were going to school in brand new squeaky shoes. Except us. The shoes couldn't have been missed by the original owners, because it wouldn't have taken a Sherlock Holmes to catch the perpetrators.

Who were the people involved in this caper of over fifty years ago? Well I'm not going to tell you. As you know, it certainly wasn't the Passes. My dad had a saying, 'If you're honest, you can show your arse in places that so-called better people dare not show theirs.'

My dad was born on 6 October 1912 in Apple Street, Neepsend. His parents, whom I never knew, were George and Martha. His brothers were Joe, Jack, Ernest and Joe Junior. Joe Junior was the son of Joe who fathered Joe Junior out of wedlock. The lady in question died in childbirth, so Joe Junior was brought up as a brother. As a kid, I wondered how I'd managed to get two Uncle Joes from the same side of the family. My dad also had two sisters, Rachel and Martha. My dad's education started at the age of thirteen and ended at the age of fourteen at Woodside School on Rutland Road.

While I grew to know his other brothers, I only remember meeting Joe Senior once. The meeting was one I wouldn't forget. Joe lived on 'the Manor' and, for a time, he was doorman at the Park and Arbourthorne Club on City Road. My dad took me along there one Sunday dinner. My dad and Joe sat down talking while I supped a bottle of pop. At one point, Joe looked at me and said, 'Close your eyes and 'old ya 'and out. Ah've got summat for thi to play wi'.' I did what I was told and, when instructed to open them, I looked in horror at what was in my hand. It was an eye. My uncle Joe's false one. I dropped it in horror, much to the amusement of Uncle Joe.

On our wall in Martin Street we had a coloured, framed picture of my grandma and my dad would often refer to her as 'The Finest', which would then cause rows between him and my mother. It was the only thing that she'd ever dream of arguing about with my dad, for she never contradicted or opposed him in any way, until grandma's name cropped up. The only time she wouldn't argue about her was New Year's Eve, because New Year's Day was grandma's birthday and my dad got really sentimental on New Year's Eve. So mother suffered in silence.

Saturday night was my dad's only night out. He and my mother would go down to the pub, the Burlington on Burlington Street, which ran across Martin Street. My brother and I would be allowed to stay up late on Saturday nights. Now and again, I'd nip out and go down to the Burlington to have a look, out of curiosity. I'd stand on the windowsill of the pub, pulling myself up by the bars on the window to peer over the half frosted glass pane. I'd see a smoke-filled room with male waiters carrying trays full of drinks, scurrying about as best they could in the packed pub. The piano would be playing, with someone singing 'Nelly Dean' and half the audience would join in. For some reason, which I couldn't understand, everybody seemed to be laughing and smiling. When my dad got home from the pub he'd be laughing too, and, for some reason, would be doing a jig and talking with an Irish accent. He'd walk in the house and say something like, 'Top of the mornin' to ya', although it would be half past ten at night. Then he'd start singing, 'If yer Irish come into the parlour, there's a welcome for you there.' My mother wore a deadpan expression of boredom (she'd probably seen the same scenario a thousand times). She'd sigh, 'Come on, you two, up them stairs,' and we'd go to bed, while dad would still be doing his Barry Fitzgerald act downstairs.

After one of these Saturday nights, I asked my mother why my dad turned into an Irishman every Saturday and she said two words, 'jungle juice', which to me meant nothing at all.

I remember once asking my dad, 'Have we any famous relations?' 'Well,' he said, 'your grandma Pass's maiden name was Lockwood and her sister started a pot business up in Sheffield. She then married a bloke called Edwards who became very well known in the rag 'n' tag market selling pots'. I then asked, 'What's that make us, then?' 'A bit potty,' he replied. Another regular thing he'd say

101

whenever Billy Cotton was on the wireless singing 'I've got a lovely bunch of coconuts' was, 'Iz 'e bragging or complaining?' But, as a little kid, I can't remember ever having a proper conversation with my dad. He'd make statements, give orders and you did it. Sometimes, he'd shout and bawl, swear and such, so much that one of my pals would comment, 'Bleeding 'ell. Ah'm glad iz not my dad'. He gave every impression of being violent, but he never hit my mother, my brother or me. Plenty of dads did in those days, but not Fred.

My dad was a big boxing fan due to the fact his dad, my granddad Joe, used to train local lads. Uncle Joe Junior became South Yorkshire schoolboy champion. My dad never rose to anything like that, but retained a certain passion for the game. He'd let me stay up for the boxing on the wireless and I'd sit with him, listening to fights that included such people as Freddie Mills and Bruce Woodcock.

One special night that stands out was when Randolph Turpin beat the legendary 'Sugar' Ray Robinson for the World Middleweight Championship. It was a result against all odds. His no-chance situation probably reminded people of the war, a sort of 'Dunkirk and still come out on top' simile. He was also living proof for the working classes that anything was possible.

A stipulation before the first fight was that, in the unlikely event that Turpin should win, he would have to defend the title against Robinson within forty days. My dad said that, if this happened, he'd have no chance in America because, as he put it, 'The Yanks'll work him a powder'. I didn't know at the time what my dad was on about but, sure enough, Turpin, a shadow of his old self, lost comprehensively in the return fight in America.

A short while after the fight, it was disclosed that two women had visited Turpin in his hotel room and some incident had occurred, which led to Turpin being accused of statutory rape. The charges were eventually dropped, but did enough to put Turpin off his objective, which was to retain his title. Was someone working Turpin a powder? We'll never know, but my dad seemed to know his boxing.

The big night for boxing on the wireless was when it came from America. Live boxing would be transmitted from Madison Square Garden and my dad and I would be up in the middle of the night, to listen to the exploits of such as Joe Louis, Ezzard Charles and Tony Zale. In fact, all the all-time greats. Just getting up with my dad at such an unearthly hour would be an adventure in itself. The next adventure would be for my dad to tune in to the required waveband. He would curse and swear at the wireless as it whistled and squeaked, while he tried to find the station. When he finally succeeded, we'd sit there staring at the wireless.

As the master of ceremonies started off with his rich American accent, 'Laydees an Gen'lemen', your brain would immediately slip into gear and your imagination would switch on. Who'd have thought, forty years later, that I'd receive a 'phone call from my sons while they were on holiday in New York, which would leave me wallowing in nostalgia. When I asked where they were calling from, one of them said, 'Somewhere called Madison Square Garden'. They asked me if I'd heard of it and my mind shot back to the Martin Street nights of me and old Fred in front of the wireless.

The only time my dad and I really sat down and talked was when he was ill with cancer. He was first diagnosed as having the disease in 1972, although he was never actually told about it. The policy now is that if you have cancer you're told, which is much better than the ignorance which was prevalent then, when the information was routinely with-held from the patient. The person they told was generally the next of kin, or another close relative, so I was the one told to make an appointment with a doctor at the Royal Infirmary on Infirmary Road. 'Your dad's got cancer,' he said. I asked if my dad had been told and the doctor said he hadn't, but that I was free to tell him. 'Or,' he went on, 'do you want me to tell him?' I said, 'No,' and asked him what my dad's chances were of beating the illness. 'Nil,' he replied. My dad died four years later on 15 March 1976 at the age of sixty-three. Up to that illness, I'd never known him to have anything more serious than a broken leg.

His all-consuming determination and attitude towards work was probably brought about by the hard times of the thirties. Later in his life, he told me what it was like to find employment in those days. When you went for a job, the first question you were asked was, 'How much would you be willing to work for?' Then, provided you suited the employers, you may sometimes have had to go through the indignity of stripping off for a medical, just like the old-time slaves. This explains why 'Land of Hope and Glory' was switched off if it ever came on the wireless in our house.

On one of my visits to him at home, while he was off sick, I'd endured a day of driving wind, sleet, snow - the lot. I'd been working outside in sub-zero temperatures and remarked to my dad that it had been lousy weather. He replied, 'No, not lousy, different. If you wake up feeling well, there's no such thing as lousy weather, just different weather.'

The last words he spoke to me were when he was in Nether Edge Hospital. He said, 'Never mind, Fred lad. Ah've 'ad two good lads, ar, two good lads.' I visited him the next night and was told by the doctor that I wouldn't be able to have a conversation with him, due to the amount of morphine they'd administered, so effectively he was dead. I'd gone to the hospital straight from work and was in my mucky working clothes and covered in dirt. As I left the hospital, I knew he was about to die. It was raining steadily and the sadness of the occasion got the better of me. Tears ran down my face. As I walked through the hospital, my path crossed a family who were jumping up and down celebrating a newborn baby. I suppose it was a classic example of the highs and lows of life.

By now the rain was really coming down and I noticed the bus parked in the terminus, so I ran as fast as I could. I got to about twenty feet from the bus. The driver looked at me, closed the doors and pulled away before I could get on. As the next bus was half an hour later, I decided to go over to the pub across the road until it came. I walked into the pub and must have looked like a big, mucky bag of wet rags. The landlord immediately declared, 'You can't come in here like that,' and suggested the dram shop if I wanted serving. I got myself a pint in the dram shop and while I was sipping it, someone put the jukebox on. It was Ella Fitzgerald singing 'Every time we say goodbye'. Tears rolled down my face again. This was obviously the final straw for the landlord. 'Come on you. Out!' He must have thought I was some sort of vagrant or a drunk because, as I left, I heard him mumble 'Bloody layabouts'.

I got home, had a bath and went to bed. The 'phone rang. It was half-past ten. I heard the voice on the other end, 'I'm sorry, your dad has passed away.' It's difficult to explain how I felt. The first feeling was of deep sadness, the second of relief because he was now free of pain, the third of guilt for feeling relieved and for ages these feelings swilled about in that order.

A few days after his death, my mother was at home, folding a pair of trousers that my dad regularly wore. In the back pocket was a note which said, 'for the grandkids'. Also in the pocket were five neat little bundles each amounting to four pounds. He must have been sat on these for ages because they were so flat they looked as if they had been ironed. The handwriting on the note was really erratic, an illustration of the amount of pain that this dreadful illness was causing him at the time. His act of thinking of someone else at a time which must have been filled with agony, sums him up. It exposed the other side of this bloke, who sometimes ranted and raved, swore and could be very bad tempered. The gesture could not have been nicer or more meaningful. It was better than some solicitor announcing a fortune had been left.

Before he died, he'd said my mother would receive four hundred pounds from the union at his final workplace, Neepsend Rolling Mills. When he could still get about, from time to time he'd visit the firm to pay his union subs. He said the bloke in charge would always say, 'Give it me another time, Fred, don't worry about it.' After his death, we received a letter of condolence from the union stating that, by the way, my mother didn't qualify for the four hundred pounds because of unpaid subs. Some condolence.

I once asked my mother why my dad didn't rise to the top job within the set of blokes he worked with, considering all the years at the Hallamshire. She told me that he had done, when I was quite small. The trouble was that when you were 'the roller', the top man on a set of ten, in those days, you'd receive papers stating how much money had been earned by the set. He'd get these papers on a Wednesday, calculate who got what, hand his calculations into the wages department on Thursday and everyone would get their money on Friday. 'The trouble was,' she said, ' that the bottom two blokes on your dad's set each had about six kids and he couldn't bring himself to pay them such a small amount of money. He used to worry how they'd manage.' She said he kept the top job for about a month but had sleepless nights so, in the end, he decided to pack the job in. As the management regarded this as a smack in the eye for them, he was reduced to being bottom man and when we got the tied house on Boyland Place, that's where he stayed.

So, make your own mind up. 'Soft as a brush' some may say but such acts leave you with a memory that all Rupert Murdoch's money couldn't buy. He'll do for me and I bet any old person, or indeed anyone who has lost someone close to them, will agree. There are some memories that just cannot be bought. As for my dad's confrontation with cancer, I've been told many times by people qualified to speak on the subject that, had my dad had his cancer ten years later, he'd have stood a seventy percent chance of beating it. It's good to know that, as time goes on, cancer sufferers needn't despair. The medical people are winning. The sooner, the better.

Chapter 15

Christmas 1951

Christmas-time in the '40s and early '50s was, as you'd expect, the highlight of the year for children. The build-up to the event was probably equal to, if not better than, Christmas itself. You'd feel the excited anticipation for a couple of weeks before, while Christmas celebrations themselves would last just two days. Christmas Day and Boxing Day. We'd start saving milk bottle tops, which would be washed, and then threaded on a line, to be hung up around the house as trimmings. They were collected with some fervour, because the more milk bottle tops you acquired, the more your house was trimmed up. Also, for a few pennies, you could buy strips of different coloured paper and make paper chains to add to your milk-bottle-top decorations.

My dad would ask me what I wanted for Christmas and pretend to write a list on a piece of paper. Then he'd hold it under the chimney in the fireplace and say, 'Let's see if he'll take our order.' He'd let go of the paper and I'd be amazed as it, apparently, vanished up the chimney, to the sounds of my dad shouting, 'He's got it!'

For years, I'd ask for the ultimate present for boys in those days, an electric train, and my dad would say, 'Ah don't think he'll 'ave any of them left.' My requests would go on until it was something affordable. Sometimes, I'd think to myself, 'I'll be down to asking for a packet of rubber bands soon.' My dad used to say that if you ordered too much you'd end up with nowt because Father Christmas had so many toys to deliver he'd never get round to all the other kids.

Christmas saw my mother bake a big spice loaf and Auntie May calling with her tiny suitcase, containing the jam tarts and mince pies that she'd made for us. She'd also bring us four or five bags of sugar which, because of rationing, was like gold dust. You could, if you wanted, use it to barter for almost anything. Auntie May's connections in the baking trade meant we were never short of sugar at Christmas.

It seemed such a busy time. My mother had her very own mobile phone - me. All sorts of messages had to be transmitted and I got the job. She'd say, 'Just nip to yer Auntie May's and tell her ...' She'd then go on for ages. I'd soak it all up and be off like a flash as soon as she'd stopped talking, and before I'd forgotten what she'd said. I didn't mind this. I jumped at any excuse to go to Auntie May's. For one thing, I never returned empty-handed and, for another, I liked asking her questions. I'd store up some pretty bizarre questions in my mind, but she never tired of them and would always attempt to give me an answer.

One perplexing question was about a drummer I'd seen in a film at the Oxford picture house. He was, it said in the film, nicknamed 'The Mad Drummer' and he looked it! He pulled all sorts of funny faces when playing the drums. I told Auntie May that he had a woman's name and asked why he pulled all those daft faces. She though a bit. 'Oh, that'll be Gene Kruper.' She went on to explain that Gene was not a woman's name. For a start, it was spelt differently

110

and in America, where he came from, Gene wasn't an uncommon name. She used the cowboy, Gene Autrey, as an example. She thought that Gene Kruper's exaggerated facial contortions were due to the fact that he was so immersed in his music. She also told me that the music fraternity had a reputation for using stimulants. I came back, inevitably, with, 'What's a stimulant?' (I must have driven her round the bend.) She pondered for a while, then said, 'Well, when your dad goes for a pint, that's a stimulant ... and you're too young to be bothering yourself about such things. Get yourself off!' So off I ran back home. I knew exactly what she meant, because my dad turned into an Irishman when he'd been to the Burlington and so I wondered if Gene Kruper spoke like an Irishman when not playing his drums.

That particular Christmas, the art teacher at Crookesmoor School, the one I called Mrs Flabbergasted - because she always looked so, well, flabbergasted - announced at assembly that there'd be a Christmas pantomime that year and the call was going out for volunteers. I was more than tempted. Auntie May had always encouraged me with, 'If you want to do it, go for it,' so that motto sprang to my mind. I was also motivated by the fact that a couple of weeks earlier, I'd stood up in our class and had them all laughing at my rendition of 'There was an old lady who swallowed a fly'. I'd tried to memorise the sequence and first performed it at home, getting it word perfect. The second time I tried it, I got it all wrong, but everyone laughed, so when the call went out on this particular day in assembly, I deliberately gave them the wrong version. They fell about laughing, too, as anticipated. It went something like 'she swallowed the cow to catch the spider that wriggled and wriggled and wriggled inside her'. When I got to the spider wriggling, I held my hands up and wriggled my fingers. I got a great round of applause for this and liked it.

My mind also reflected on all the films that I'd seen, countless times, in all sorts of picture houses - The Oxford, The Western, The Unity, The Scala, even The News Theatre in Fitzalan Square in town. Added to this, I'd been to Blackpool with Auntie May and seen the likes of Wilfred Pickles, Al Read, Joseph Locke and Donald Peers. I felt like a veteran of the stage. The films I'd seen were always watched from the front row, because I thought, 'the closer, the better.' I'd seen the big red velvet curtains open and shut half a dozen times when Joseph Locke brought his show to an end with his rendition of 'Goodbye' at Blackpool. So, with all my stage experience, I felt confidant when I turned up for Mrs Flabbergasted's casting meeting after school.

The pantomime was to be Aladdin and His Magic Lamp. The prospective actors sat on the floor in a semi-circle while Mrs Flabbergasted wafted around with a load of papers in her hand. She was a big, fattish woman who had a permanent blush on her face and always seemed to be perspiring and dabbing her forehead with a hanky she kept up her sleeve, all the time demonstrating her 'flabbergasted' label. She went on an on about how all the kids could sell tickets and, straight away, I thought of Auntie May, Uncle Ern, and mam and dad, all in the audience, looking on proudly. I knew in advance that Dennis, Jenks and Pete would 'ave me on' but I soon dismissed this from my mind. It would be a small price to pay for instant stardom. Hollywood beckoned and, aged eight, I couldn't wait. Mrs Flabbergasted gave us all a rough gist of the pantomime and said that rehearsals would start the following week.

I sat there musing. Aladdin. Just the job. I was perfect for the part. Mrs Flabbergasted said that all speaking parts had to be learned as quickly as possible and that she'd hand out the scripts to the characters, one by one. Each potential star had to stand as she announced them. We all had to applaud and she gave them the script. Just the ticket. Applause just for standing up.

She started off with Aladdin, then worked her way down the parts. I sat clapping my hands off for everybody, until there was no one left but me. Mrs Flabbergasted looked down on me. 'Now then, Freddie, how would you like a non-speaking part as a passer by?' 'A what?!' 'A passer-by,' she repeated, 'It's an important part that would involve two or three costume changes.' 'So I wouldn't be recognised as being the same passer-by in different scenes,' I thought to myself. Who wants to be in a pantomime and not be noticed? It would be like Joseph Locke singing behind the big red velvet curtains instead of in front.

'Ah want a talking part,' I declared, putting my cards on the table. 'Well, Freddie, after hearing your rendition of "There was an Old Lady who Swallowed A Fly" I've come to the conclusion that you would have difficulty remembering the words in the right order.' I quickly defended myself. 'Oh that! I said t'words wrong on purpose to gerra laff.' On hearing this, her flabber was really gasted. 'You mean you deliberately said that little ditty out of sequence just to get attention and show off?' 'Well, ar. Ah thought if tha wor in a show, tha '*ad* to show off. '

At this she really went up the wall, making wailing sounds like Mrs Aistrop did when giving birth. 'Don't you "thee" and "tha" to me young man,' she bellowed, 'Get out of this room at once. I'll be telling your teacher about such behaviour.' The last part of her rebuke translated as, 'I'm not going to hit you with a stick, but I know someone who will'.

So, something that I'd felt confident about and really looked forward to, had been turned upside down. I was in trouble and couldn't understand why. The casting night was a Friday night and I thought that, by Monday, it would have all been forgotten. No such luck. Before the lessons started for the day, the teacher, who obviously had been primed by Mrs Flabbergasted, had me standing in front of the class while he went on about the pitfalls of showing off. He said that I had conned the whole school with my deliberate, out of sequence 'There was an Old Lady' routine. I couldn't help thinking, 'Ah must be a good actor, then, if they all fell for it.' He said he wouldn't put up with show-offs in his class and that I'd been disrespectful towards a lady and I'd pay the price. 'Hold your hand out, boy.' He always stopped calling you by name when he was about to cane you. He then brought his cane down. *Whack*. I screwed my hand up after the impact. He then gave me a shove in the back towards my seat, saying curtly, 'Sit down.' I winced with pain and fought back a tear as I walked to my seat. With all the other kids staring at me, I wasn't going to cry. Then, the day started. One two is two, two twos are four.

When I got home, Auntie May had been with the jam tarts

and mince pies. After she had gone, my mother placed them on the table. She also added the spice loaf she'd baked plus apples, oranges, nuts, bananas, figs and dates. Happiness shone on her face. 'Just look at this lot Freddie, dunt it look smashin'?' 'Ar,' I replied. She then went to the cupboard and got out a big old empty biscuit tin and put a few of almost everything in it. She cut a chunk off the spice loaf and put that in. Also a bag of sugar. 'What ya doin', mam?' 'Shut up and put thi shoes on.' She put the lid on the, now full, biscuit tin. 'Take these to Mrs Aistrop and ask her to send me the tin back when she's done with it.' I knew no better, at my age, and just thought she was going chuffing daft, giving all that food away. But my mother was no martyr. Her act was typical of the people of the times, a thing that makes those times special.

Well, back to Christmas morning. I looked in my pillow case to find a Beano annual, a snakes and ladders game with a label on from Auntie May, a blow-football game from Uncle Ernest, an apple and an orange, six brand new pennies wrapped in tissue paper and a plastic football. Added to this, downstairs, all the house was trimmed up, there was food on the table, a visit from Auntie May and Uncle Ern guaranteed (hopefully, separate visits), and my mam and dad smiling for two whole days! To top all this off, my dad wouldn't be at work. I didn't mind him being Irish for a couple of days, even though I couldn't tell what he was talking about for most of the time. Christmas was a truly happy time. Getting the cane for the pantomime fiasco soon faded. Anyway, things seemed so good, I thought, 'Who wants to be in t'pantomime anyway?'

Chapter 16

Uncle Ern

Auntie May, on my mother's side, and Uncle Ern, on my dad's side, were two very special people to me, both as a kid and as a grown-up. I could never understand how I could like two people who were opposite in every way, especially as it was obvious that they didn't think much of each other. If ever they visited our house at the same time, there would be an uneasy silence.

Uncle Ernest was the youngest of my dad's brothers.   He lived a stone's throw away from us on Martin Lane, with his wife Nelly, who was a fussy little thing. As a child, I was always reminded of a butterfly. She seemed to be forever fluttering around, not doing anything in particular, though she was very pleasant to me, as I'm sure she was with everyone else.

Ernest was a bloke of stocky build, about five feet eight inches tall with light brown wavy hair which he kept combed back, the style of the times, I suppose. Ernest was a happy-go-lucky character who always wore a smile, didn't give a toss for any sort of authority, and was always out and about and going somewhere or other.

Ernest had been captured by the Germans during the war and had spent over four years as a prisoner kept in various prison camps in Poland, among other places, and this was probably the reason for his attitude towards life. Around that time, a typical scene on a winter's night in Martin Street, would be my mother and me sat listening to a magician or, even worse, a juggler, on the wireless. It'd be dark and cold outside. My mind would be wondering, thinking about our next post-a-cat venture or something along those lines. Then I'd hear the sound of somebody's 'walk'. Ernest always had segs in his shoes so, if a 'seggy' walk had an accompanying whistle, I knew it was Uncle Ern. My ears would prick up and my mother would say, 'It sounds like Ernest.' This was a signal to me to reach up to turn off the wireless because I didn't want to miss a word he said, but, invariably, my mother would stop me. 'Don't turn it off, I'm listening to that juggler.'

In would walk Ern. To me he was a latter day Indiana Jones and James Bond rolled into one. He always referred to me by the German version of my name, Friedrich, and would tell me stories of how he was captured by the Germans and how he 'took out' twelve of them first, how he was sentenced to a firing squad, but reprieved at the last moment by the Field Marshall, as a mark of respect from the Germans. He'd a thousand and one stories that would keep me amused. Ernest's stories made him an illusionist and there was plenty of room for one on Martin Street.

Compared to our wireless, he faced no competition. In the middle of one of his stories, he'd often suddenly stop and say, 'Does tha fancy gooin' tut Western?' The Western was a local picture house on St Phillip's Road. It was aptly named, for westerns were the films most likely to be showing. Did I want to go? What a question. One minute bored out of my mind, the next transported to the ultimate night out, a night at the pictures along with Uncle Ern. 'Yeah!' I'd shout. He'd say, 'Tha'd better ask thi mam first.' So I'd shout, 'Canna mam? Canna?' She'd reply, 'Ah suppose so,' and Uncle Ern and I would be off.

On one such visit to the pictures, he gave me a bag of Brazil nuts. I asked how I was supposed to eat them. 'Easy. Wi these,' and gave me a pair of nutcrackers. As I started to crack the nuts during the picture show, heads started to turn in annoyance at the noise that was distracting them from the film, so I stopped for a while until Ernest asked, 'What's up, dunt tha like em?' 'Arr, but …' 'Ne'er mind "but", gerrem etten if tha likes 'em.' So, rather nervously, I carried on cracking the nuts, waiting in trepidation for the consequences.

Sure enough, some bloke turned round and said to Ernest,

'A tha gonna stop that young un wi them nuts?'
'No, Ah'm not.'
'Ah can't 'ear chuffin' picture.'
'If tha dunt like it, shift' - an' if tha dunt want to shift, let's me and thee gu outside and thi'll be moor than nuts crackin'.'

The bloke shifted. I mused that, afterwards, I'd be able to tell my pals about it, saying, 'Everybody's freetund o' Uncle Ern.'

He once turned up at our house with a set of fishing tackle, junior size. He said he'd bought it off a bloke as a favour and, seeing that it was no good to him, 'Tha might as well have 'em.' So, you could add Father Christmas to the list of characters he embodied. He'd often turn up, out of the blue, to ask if I'd fancy going to Boston or some other fishing place. A day's fishing would always be one to remember.

118

One particular excursion to Boston turned out to be a trip and a half. We were fishing by the river and, by the side, was an orchard surrounded by a big high fence. There was a bloke in the orchard, tending his apples. Alongside him were two Alsatian dogs. Ernest suddenly put down his fishing tackle and motioned me to go with him, gesticulating towards the apple man. So, I, too, left my rod and we approached the bloke and his dogs, who were in the orchard inside the fence. Immediately, the dogs start snarling and barking, so Ernest had a chat to the bloke, in a passing-the-time-of-day sort of fashion and finished off his chat with, 'Does tha ever get any apples pinched?' 'No chance, not with these two', replied the bloke, referring to the dogs. 'They'd rip anybody to pieces given half a chance.' Ernest bade the bloke 'good-day' and, on our way back to our fishing, said to me in a confidential tone, 'Well tha's gonna get some pinched today, owd lad.' 'But Uncle Ern, tha'll get ripped to pieces.' Ernest just laughed. 'Shurrup wi thee.'

An hour or so later Ernest announced, 'Reight, Ah'm off. Thee just concentrate on thi fishin' and don't turn round.' Off he went with a haversack that had previously held fishing equipment. I sat there looking at the float in the river, listening for screams and barking dogs. Not a sound. About half an hour later, Ernest returned with the haversack full of apples.' 'Ere thi are, Friedrich. Get stuck into them. What tha dunt eat, gee to thi mam and dad, but don't sey owt.' In all probability, Ernest had bought the apples, but that wouldn't have crossed my mind at the time.

Later, after the fishing, Ernest told me that he knew a woman who lived in Boston and we'd be paying her a visit because

119

he'd heard that she was having trouble with her bedroom wallpaper. When we got to this house, she seemed really pleased to see Uncle Ern. He told her that I was hungry, so she prepared tea for me. Boiled ham, tomatoes, tea, bread and butter, a plate of cakes and buttered malt loaf. 'Aren't you having any tea, Uncle Ern?' I asked. 'No,' said Ernest, 'I've got that wallpaper upstairs to sort out haven't Ah,' looking at the woman. 'Oh, yes,' she confirmed. So, off they went upstairs, while I got stuck into, what seemed at the time, a very posh tea. Loud noises started coming from upstairs. 'Uncle Ern's really getting stuck into the wallpapering job,' I thought. I occasionally heard the woman exclaim, 'Oh.' 'I bet Uncle Ern's gone and ripped some wallpaper,' I surmised. Anyway, they eventually came downstairs and, by the look her face, he'd done a smashing job. She waved us goodbye, shouting to Ernest, 'You know where I live, if you're ever around these parts.'

As we were walking to the railway station Ernest said to me, 'Ya know what hardest thing int prison camps were?' 'What?' I asked. 'Keeping secrets,' Ernest said. 'Oh,' said I. He went on, 'No-one back home knows Ah'm good at wallpapering and if thi find aaht Ah'll end up wallpapering every neet ot week. So tha keeps it a secret. O tha listening, Friedrich?' 'Course Ah will, Uncle Ern, Ah'll not tell nob'dy',' I say and we proceeded to the railway station.

We got to the station only to find out we'd missed the last train due to Ernest's diligence. What we gonna do, Uncle Ern, what we gonna do?' I asked in trepidation. 'Wi'll walk it back,' says Ern, 'It's on'y up rooad'. I thought, 'Up rooad, it must be a thousand mile away.' So, with the time about seven o'clock, we started walking back to Sheffield. On the way, Ernest kept me entertained with his concentration camp adventures. Also, he was covered in tattoos from neck to ankle, front and back, and each one had a story attached to it.

We hitched rides on all sorts of vehicles and finally got a lift on the back of a half-loaded lorry of potatoes. We were dropped off in Worksop, got a bus from there and finally walked up Martin Street about midnight. My mother and dad were looking anxiously down the street.

'Weer the chuffin' 'ell have tha been?' asked dad. 'Missed last train,' said Ern. 'How'd ya manage that?' 'Young Friedrich wo catching so many fish wi cunt drag usselves away, could wi?' said Uncle Ern, while looking down at me. 'No,' I confirmed. Uncle Ern ruffled my hair and said, 'Thaz gorra good lad there, Fred. Goodnight, all,' and was off into the darkness, whistling as he went.

Years later, in my teens, I asked my dad if Ernest was good at wallpapering. He gave me a puzzled look, ' 'E's never wall-papered in his life. What makes thi ask that?' 'Oh nowt,' I said. Well, it **was** a secret.

As I grew up, I realised that Ernest had become a very lonely bloke and, even when I was in my thirties he was, sadly, still telling me his old wartime escapades. I continued to listen out of respect, but was filled with sadness for the bloke who had been such a godsend to the little scruffy kid from Martin Street.

I remember being told that, on returning home from the war, Ernest arrived back in Sheffield unannounced, so he though he would pay a visit to his dad's grave in Burngreave Cemetery. It was early morning and the graveyard was locked up, so Ernest scaled the railings and found his dad's grave, only to discover that while he had been away his mother had died, too. Some homecoming.

Ernest died of cancer at the age of sixty and was cremated at City Road Cemetery. As they brought his coffin into the church, someone whispered, 'It's a shame he had no kids.' They didn't know it, but he had. Me. To this day, if I close my eyes I can hear his walk and his whistle and that's another memory that's not for sale.

Chapter 17

It's enough to make you think

I was walking up Martin Street, one day, with my mother, on our way to the shops. On the other side of the road was a woman walking in the opposite direction, dressed all in black, with her eyes fixed straight ahead. She passed people without giving them a glance or stopping to have a natter which, for Martin Street, was unusual. It was probably the nattering capital area of Yorkshire.

In true Martin Street fashion, my mother stopped to talk to some woman going in the opposite direction, on our side of the road, and the subject of their nattering was the woman in black. She looked a bit scary to me, so I was all ears. 'It's a shame ya know,' said my mother. 'Ah know, she's never been the same since she lost their Colin,' said the other woman. 'Ar,' agreed my mother, 'he were only 19.' The other continued, 'and weren't 'e a nice lad? Always smiling.' 'They reckon 'e wurra good worker, 'he'd gorra job dahn Attercliffe somewhere an't he?' my mother asked. 'Ah think so,' the other confirmed, '... Anyway, Ah'll 'ave to be off Gladys, ar Bert'll think Ah've bin stud abaht natterin'.' Which was exactly what she had been doing. As the natterer walked away, my mother shouted after her, 'Wi don't 'no' 'ow lucky we are.'

I used to see the sad woman quite often and couldn't help but stand and stare at her. I thought she looked like some kind of ghost. To all effects, she probably was - the walking, breathing, talking variety. I always felt sorry for her. When you think of the hardships of the times - slum houses, limited food, terrible working conditions - she had an extra burden to carry. The loss of her only son in the war.

I once asked my dad, what would have happened to us if Hitler had won the war and he said, ' 'E'd 'ave probably looked at us lot, seen 'ow we were dressed, where we were living, an' razed Martin Street tut ground.'

The memory of that woman is one I'll never forget. Years later, when my wife, Sandra, and I were on a coach holiday to Germany, we stopped for an hour at a roadside café somewhere in Belgium. After spending a short while in the café, I decided to have a stroll around. About ten yards up the road there was a white gate ajar, I strolled through it, to be faced by a well-manicured grass banking. I walked up it to have a look what was on the other side. The sight that suddenly greeted me caused a feeling to well up in my stomach, up through my throat and forced out an involuntary, 'Oh!' I'd stumbled on a war cemetery. Lines and lines of white crosses for as far as the eye could see. I thought of the old lady in black and Colin, the lad she'd lost. I stood there looking at thousands and thousands of Colins without whom, to use my dad's words, 'E would 'ave razed Martin Street tut ground.' I looked at the names and ages. Joseph So-and-so, aged twenty-one, Albert So-and-so, aged twenty. Every name, every age you could think of. During my early childhood, I was ignorant of these sad facts of life. My mind was on other matters.

If, on television I ever see little black lads running about playing football in terrible surroundings, I can really identify with them. That was us. One thing that hits you is that they're enjoying it, despite all their obvious problems. We did, too. All we needed was space and a ball. Our main area for football was the tip at the top of Martin Street. The top pitch ran north-south and the lower one, east-west. I was really hooked on football and soon learned the unwritten code of conduct. You didn't moan if you were hurt and you didn't dispute any decisions for, if you did, you'd be called 'mardy arse'. You didn't brag about any goals you scored or anything good you'd done or you'd become a 'big eard'. A little kid who portrayed any of these traits was put down quickly.

The big lads, aged fourteen and over, mainly played on the top pitch. The main game was probably Martin Street versus Mushroom Lane. There were some good footballers around that area - the Pooles, Wasdens, Havenhands, Cars, Mortons, and many more. Temporary goal posts would be erected. They were kept in Ernest Morton's yard, which happened to be the last yard before reaching the pitch at the top of Martin Street. The ball would be kept well 'dubbined' in an old onion bag. It was treasured like a latter day Holy Grail. There'd be some bloke or other who'd be present at these matches with a bag, not to tend to injured players. His sole concern was the ball. His job was vital for the plain fact was there **was** only one ball. So, no ball, no football. It was as simple as that. In his bag, he'd have dubbin to keep the ball weather-proof, a large darning needle, cat gut scissors, a pen knife and a lacer for lacing the ball. He should have added a Bible in case any of these tools failed.

The ball would often collapse through old age and this bloke would dash on with his bag of tricks. If a crowd of players gathered round he'd wave them away with flailing arms, indicating he wanted space to perform 'the operation'. The players, hands on hips, would look to the heavens or pace around like expectant fathers, waiting for the result of 'the operation'. The bloke, after completing his task, would bounce the ball to signify all was well. There would then be a huge sigh of relief from the players and a huge cheer from the crowd, which sometimes consisted of several hundred. The bouncing of the ball signalled 'game on'.

Of all the football grounds in the world, I'd have loved to play on the top pitch of the tip. I never managed it because we left Martin Street before I was old enough. Calling it a 'pitch' may seem daft because the pitch itself was totally devoid of any grass, and was aptly named the 'tip'.

My first visit to a proper football ground was during the 1949-50 season, or it may have been 1950-51. Mrs Hogg, who lived in the corner of our yard, took me to Hillsborough, along with her son Frank, to see Sheffield Wednesday play Manchester United. As we approached the ground, I was full of excitement and anticipation. From the top of Leppings Lane, the Wednesday ground looked like a giant hoover and all the people looked like lumps of muck getting sucked in. My pace quickened. I just couldn't wait to get sucked in. Once inside, it was awesome to me. I'd never seen so many people in one place before. The noise they made when the teams ran out was scary at first. The colours - red shirts of Manchester and the blue and white of Wednesday and the lush green colour of the grass - a truly unforgettable occasion. The result was Wednesday nil, Manchester United four. Ah well, some things don't change. I got home from the match and said to my dad, 'It were great but nobdy's gooin' next week. Thi all sed Wednesday's rubbish.' My dad just laughed and I wondered why.

Bonfire Night in Martin Street was always a good demonstration of the strong sense of community that our family and neighbours shared. Most yards had their own bonfire. All the rubbish would be piled up in the centre of the yard and, complete with Guy Fawkes, it would be set alight around six o'clock in the evening and would go on until around eleven. All the kids and women would sit together chattering and all the men would sit round having a bottle of beer. There'd be chestnuts and potatoes on the fire, and the distinct lack of fireworks didn't detract from what was usually a smashing night.

The Bonfire Night we had when I was about seven years old stands out in my memory because something awful happened which made me realise there was a nasty, cruel world outside the kind, supportive one I knew. It was to be my first sight of real violence. A family came from another yard to join in the festivities. Everything was going fine, the men were drinking their beer, the women were nattering and the kids were laughing and running around. Then some bloke announced, 'All ale's gone.' There were a few moans of, 'Oh bleedin' 'ell' and other suitable phrases of disappointment. The husband of the family that had joined us shouted, 'Dunt matter lads. I've a crateful dahn our cellar,' and dashed off up our entry to fetch it. On his way back down the entry there was a bump as he collided with the wall, followed by a few choice words. Dennis and I glanced at each other. The bloke didn't seem to mind. He'd probably felt nothing, because of the effects of the beer. Anyway, he shrugged it off and, with a big smile, said, 'Come on lads, get stuck into this lot.' He opened one bottle, tried to pour it into someone's glass and nothing came out. So now he's not smiling. He inspected the others, from time to time glancing across the yard at his wife and kids. When he found another empty, he started to remove his leather belt and wrap part of it around his fist. At this, his wife jumped up holding her hands to her mouth. He walked across to her and lashed her on her back with the belt. She screamed and made a dash for the entry. The bloke chased her, hitting her time and time again, as hard as he could, while she was running and screaming, the bloke shouting, 'Gerrin that fuckin' house.'

Some of the kids were crying at the sight. I was in total shock, but the bloke's kids were not crying - or in shock. They'd seen it all before. My mother shouted to my dad, 'Stop him, Fred.' He dashed off and, after a while, the three of them came back. The sobbing woman was comforted by the rest of the women and the bloke carried on drinking and laughing as though nothing had happened despite the fact that, as far as the others were concerned, it was clear he was no longer regarded as one of the crowd.

When the bonfire was finally out, I couldn't help wondering what went on when they got home and there was no one to stop him. My dad could look a fearsome figure at times and could be bad tempered. He certainly used to swear a lot, but he never hit anyone. My dad's saying was 'violence breeds violence'.

I was certainly faced with new experiences during those

years. The next was a real eye-opener.

The first black people in Sheffield came to live nearby around that time. I think there were about a dozen or so of them living in big, old dilapidated Victorian houses down Oxford Street. At the first sight of them, I was really scared. The only other black people I'd seen were those with spears in their hands in Tarzan films. They seemed to walk sort of funny, taking deliberate steps, as though it hurt their feet when they touched the ground.

After the first sighting, I dashed home. For once, my dad was in. 'Dad, thiz some blackies on Oxford Street!' 'So what? Thi on'y same as us, so don't you go botherin' 'em.' ' 'Ow iz it thi black, then?' My dad, never one to elaborate, said, 'It's just cuz thiv been int sun a lot.' Anyway, pretty soon they were integrated into the community and you'd see them at the Oxford Pictures and in all the other places in the neighbourhood.

They hadn't been there long when Dennis, Pete and I were walking up Oxford Street and we were hit by a lovely smell coming from one of the immigrant's houses. We must have looked like the Bisto Kids, with our noses in the air. We traced the smell to one of the houses where the front window was shoved up. On a tray were toffee apples displaying a sign 'Toffee Apples One Penny'. We all dashed off to mither our mothers' lives out for the penny needed. After pestering a bit, we all dashed back up to Oxford Street clutching our coins.

So, the only problem then was who was going to go to the window to do the buying. Dennis and I decided it should be Pete, what with him being the smallest. Pete said, 'Ah'm not,' so we gave him a few rounds of, 'Th'art freetund.' That didn't work. 'Yor gu then.' So all three of us were stuck there. We'd got the money for the toffee apples, but not the nerve to fetch them. Then, Dennis, thinking logically as usual, reasoned, 'We're not nicknamed Look, Duck and Vanish for nowt and no-one yet has caught us all.' So we decided we'd all go together. Brave as anything, we marched up to the window, Dennis and me behind Pete. When we got to the window, the woman produced a big white smile and said, 'Hello mi little darlings, and what can a do for you?' 'Can we' ave a toffee apple?' we all said, in unison. 'You certainly can, mi little loves, and I'll tell you what, seein' as you are my first customers al give ya the biggest.' As she was sorting out the biggest, we noticed a bloke standing about behind her, who, I guessed, was her husband. She took our money and handed us the toffee apples saying, 'Bye bye, mi little chickens.' As we turned round thinking, 'She's reight enough,' the bloke shouted through the window, 'Quick, grab 'em for the pot.' At this, we dashed down the path, screaming our heads off. The bloke was laughing helplessly and the woman was hitting him with a tea towel, saying, 'We'll never sell any, doing things like that.' The bloke was still laughing and we were thinking, 'Chuffin 'ell, that wor a close call.'

Apart from being black, the only difference from the rest of the neighbours was that they smiled a lot and, for my part, I never heard a word of resentment or word against them, ever, for if black meant you were at the bottom of the pile, we were all black on Martin Street.

Chapter 18

Out and about

During the six week holidays, sometimes, when we had nothing to do, half a dozen of us would scrape together a penny each and catch the circular bus on Crookesmoor Road and travel all round Sheffield, just for somewhere to go. Depending on the conductor, for a penny, you could stop on the bus all day. Other times, we'd go to the museum in Weston Park, not that any of us had any interest in anything in there, but it was free and, again, it was somewhere to go.

There was one attendant there who, at the sight of us, would follow us around, about three or four yards behind. We noticed that, when we stopped, he stopped, when we walked slowly, he did. So this began to be a bit of a game. We'd all walk quickly then suddenly change to a very slow march. We'd go up the stairs and when we got there, turn round and come back down again, only to turn round and go back up, all the time followed by this suspicious sod who was making life hard for himself. And we were all doing our best to help him. This game sometimes went on for ages until we'd decide to split up. His nerves would snap and he'd order us all out of the building.

But the thing that we all really liked was a night at the pictures. We'd take empty bottles back to the shop to raise the needed amount and, some way or other, get the required ninepence or whatever it was. Sometimes, there'd be as many as ten of us all, on the front row the 'The Pit' (cheapest part) of the Oxford, just off Oxford Street. We sometimes took a bottle of water in a non-returnable type of bottle with screwed up newspaper bunged in the top of it as the stopper. We'd all stare up at the cowboys out in the boiling sun on the range and pass on the bottle to each other for a quick swig. I suppose it was a sort of front-runner of virtual reality.

Anyway, these pictures used to nearly always end up with the cavalry coming to someone's rescue when there seemed no hope at all. At the sound of the distant bugle, that told everyone help was on its way, we all started cheering. At the end of the film, the doors would be flung open and the cold air rushed in. Then, up on the screen would be a fluttering Union Jack, and the national anthem would play. Most people stood until the anthem had finished. Not us, we'd be off. Sometimes, grown ups grumbled, 'Stay where you are, ya little buggers.' No chance. We'd be running out of the door, all slapping our arses and riding imaginary horses in the re-enactment of what we'd just seen. Our heroes were Durango Kid, Hopalong Cassidy, Randolph Scott, Lash Larue, The 'Cisco Kid and many more. Tarzan and Sabu were other favourites. I've been them all.

One Tarzan film had me particularly puzzled. Tarzan's English was very poor - 'me Tarzan you Jane' sort of stuff - and I thought, 'Tha'd 'av' a reight job 'avin' a chat wi 'im.' Anyway, in this film, these white blokes told Tarzan they were looking for the elephant's graveyard to do a zoological study. (They, too, had sussed that old Tarzan was a bit thick, due to his limited chat-up lines.) Anyway, Tarzan replied, 'Only people who know elephant graveyard is Mogombi Tribe. They never see white man before. I take you.'

We were all sitting there on the front row thinking, 'Daft chuff is kiddin' thi, Tarzan.' This was especially obvious because the leader of the white blokes spoke with a German accent and, to top it all, had a scar on his cheek. He was obviously a villain.

So, Tarzan's chopping his way through all kinds of undergrowth, all the time being watched by mysterious eyes, peeking at the explorers through the extensive flora. The picture faded out two or three times to emphasise the perils of the journey.

Pete declared, 'He's bleedin' daft, doin' all that for nowt.' 'Shurrup!' we snapped back. Dennis nudged me. 'Pass water. It's mekking me thirsty, all this jungle stuff.' They finally reached 'The Tribe', who had never seen a white man before, and there was the chief sitting on a big throne. He was as black as soot, weighed about twenty stone, and had a big club in his hand and a bone through his nose. Tarzan approached and this chief, who'd never, other than Tarzan, seen a white man before, greeted Tarzan with, 'Hiya Tarzan, what canna do for ya.' His accent was reminiscent of James Cagney's.

My mother once took me to see Casablanca, probably on its tenth trip around the picture houses. A classic film, but it bored the life out of me. It probably just shaded stopping in to watch the wireless. To occupy my mind, I looked for things that didn't seem right.

Humphrey Bogart was running 'Rick's Place' in Casablanca

and in walked an old flame of his, Ingrid Bergman. He hadn't seen her for about ten years, and that was about ten thousand miles away, yet Humphrey swung into his, 'Of all the gin joints in all the world' routine. I was thinking, if that was me, I'd say something like, 'Chuffin' ell, wot thar doin' 'ere?'

In another part of the film, Paul Heinreid tells old Ingrid, who he's married to, that he's off out to do a bit of espionage or something and she's whittled to death, telling him to be careful, as Casablanca is full of Nazis. He reassures her that he'll be okay and won't be seen because it's in the middle of the night. He opens the curtains (as if she doesn't know what time of day it is) to show her it's pitch black outside. Then he gives her a kiss and sets off in his white suit and to top it all, a white fedora. I'm thinking, 'No wonder Germans lost war if they didn't notice a bloke skipping about in a white suit and fedora in the middle of the night in Casablanca.'

In those days, most of the films had thin plots. The actors were typecast, but people queued in their hundreds to see them. Anything was better than sitting in the house with nothing to do.

That was exactly what I was doing one day when my mother said, 'Oh, that sound's like the ragman ont street.' She gave me a bundle of rags with the order, 'Get me a lump of donkey stone,' so off I dashed with the bundle. Our ragman had the look of John Mills in 'Ryan's Daughter'. I saw the film years and years later and wondered who he reminded me of. It didn't take long before it came to me. He looked as if he'd been put together with bits and pieces of other people, and his eyes looked in different directions. Well, this particular day, I gave him the rags and he asked, 'What's tha want?'

'What's tha got?' He trotted out the usual selection of cups, windmills (a stick with a flower-shaped paper effort on the top that would whiz round if it ever got windy - babies sometimes had them stuck on their prams), donkey stone, pegs and goldfish. 'Ah'll tek a goldfish.' When I got back to the house, my mother sighed. 'Ah thought Ah teld thi to get mi some donkey stone?' "E'd on'y got goldfish,' I replied as innocently as I could. Well, we had a little goldfish bowl in our bottom cupboard and I'd reasoned to myself that there was no use having a goldfish bowl and no goldfish, so my conscience was clear and, anyway, it would brighten the house up for mother. A couple of days later, Pete came over. 'Can Ah look at thi goldfish?' By this time, the fish was floundering about a bit, probably due to the diet of Paxo stuffing I'd been feeding it (when my mother wasn't looking). Pete was obviously interested in the fish.

'What's tha call it?'
'Doreen.'
'Ars tha know it's a lass?'
'Ragman teld mi.'
'Ars he know?'
'Shurrup ya little twat. Does tha want to look at her or what?'
'It looks like it's deein' to me.'
'It won't in a bit.'

Then I went to the drawer and got out a tablespoon and gave the water a big swizz. Old Doreen was whizzing round like nobody's business. Pete got to the door. His closing comment was,

'It still looks like it's deein' to me,' and dashed off. I think Doreen lasted three days, but she was still better than a lump of donkey stone.

Later on that week, I was dashing up Martin Street, only to be suddenly dragged back by my shirt collar. This lad, who was about sixteen, we'll call him Johnny Big Gob, had grabbed me and said, while pointing to some lasses on the corner, 'Goo an' ask her wit green frock on to go out wi mi tomorra night.' 'Ask 'er thissen,' I shouted back. Still holding me, he gave me a clip on the back of the head, 'Don't thee get smart wi me, Passey.' 'What's in it for me?' I asked. 'A threp'ny bit, if she sez no, and a bob if she sez aar.' So off I went.

'Johnny sez will ya goo aart wi' 'im tomorra?' 'Ah've arranged to meet Rita at Roscoe at seven, but in any case Ah wunt go out wi' 'im. He must be a reight nelly if he dernt ask issen. Tell 'im to piss off,' she hissed back. Then she went on her way, up the street with her mates. I went back to Big Gob. He had a threepenny bit in one hand, and a bob in the other. 'Come on, Passey, which one's it gonna be?' He held them both out, one in each hand. I grabbed the bob and said, 'She'll see thi outside Roscoe at seven.' He pulled his shirt collar up. 'Ah knew it, bleedin' mad abart mi.'

The next day, I told Dennis and Pete about Johnny's imaginary date and they were well chuffed because this kid had a habit of scutching kids just for the fun of it. We decided to go down to the Roscoe to witness Johnny Big Gob being brought down to earth. We hid behind a pub opposite. Dennis organised the timing and we are there for twenty to seven. We peeked across to the

Roscoe. 'Bleedin' 'ell, Passey, 'e's already waitin',' Pete hissed. Well all fell about laughing. Smart arse Johnny was waiting for this lass and he was going to get a huge shock in a bit and we couldn't wait. By the time it got to five to seven, Rita was on the other corner, waiting for the lass who Johnny thought he was taking out. Dennis had a good vantage point and suddenly snorted, 'He's wearing a cravat!' Pete misheard this and replied, 'What's he wearing a carrot fo'?' I hissed, 'Not a carrot, a cravat.' ' 'E looks like Noel Coward,' Dennis added. 'He'll bleedin' kill thi, Passey, if he catches thi.' By this time, we were almost pissing ourselves in true Look, Duck and Vanish tradition, as Johnny constantly brushed down the front and sleeves of his coat. Nerves.

Our escape routes were planned in advance, because it was important that Johnny saw us. Humiliation was the name of the game and we had a few lines of a song we wanted to sing to him before we disappeared. Pete spotted her first. 'She's 'ere.' We could see her before Johnny, which made it better. She was walking towards the Roscoe, all frizzy-hair and done up, wearing a neckerchief, with the ends sticking out to one side. 'Way, she's bleedin' 'orrible,' said Pete and, not being old enough to appreciate the female anatomy, added, 'All' er chest's wobblin' abart. Urrgh.' Then as she got to Big Gob, he took a step forward and smiled.

She frowned and walked past him, threw her head to one side, saying what looked like, 'Piss off', met her friend, and into the pictures they went.

Johnny frowned and looked totally shattered. He glanced from side to side, not knowing what to do. Then, with perfect timing, we jumped out from across the road and started singing, 'I was standing on the corner of the street, in case a certain little lady goes by.' The last few words were spat out very quickly because he was like a mad bull, trying to get across the road to us, or should I say, me.

We'd worked out that Pete would run right, Dennis left and I'd go just straight in the opposite direction. They would delay their run to just a few seconds after me, just to confuse him. Ideally, he'd want to catch me and would be confused by the 'different timing and different directions' plan. It was me he would want. It was me who had took his bob (and had spent it), so the song was hardly finished when I was off in a straight direction over Bow Bridge, then turned left on Neepsend Lane to Rutland Bridge. Just as Rutland Bridge finished, there was a narrow walkway that led you to the back of the works by the River Don. Left again, down an alleyway and out you came to, yes, the Roscoe.

Well, my heart was pounding as I set off. I looked over my shoulder. If he didn't hesitate and concentrated on me, I'd be in trouble. He'd have a good chance of catching me. As I looked over my shoulder, Johnny had stopped. Then he took a few steps after Dennis, a few steps after Pete, a couple of seconds before he decided to chase me. So, it worked. We all met up where we had started. My heart was still pounding with the excitement and Little Pete said, oh so seriously, 'What shall wi do naah?'

That was nearly over fifty years ago and I haven't seen Johnny since.

Chapter 19

A sign of the times

Boredom was probably responsible for our mischievous-ness, from time to time, a sort of last resort. One way to combat the boredom of dark winter evenings was to traipse around with a bundle of old comics that you'd read a dozen times. Such comics were never thrown away. They'd be saved to swap. I'd often go up and down all the cobbled streets around Martin Street knocking on doors with the enquiry, 'Has your Arnold got any comics to swap?' or something like that. You could spend a couple of hours doing this and, if you were lucky, end up with three or four comics, which, although might be a little torn and tattered, would be new to you, assuming you'd not read them before. So, comics were never thrown away. They became a sort of kids' currency, a valuable defence against the boredom of winter nights and, most importantly, the exercise cost nowt.

On my travels around the dark and dingy streets, the only source of lighting, except for the dull glow from houses, were gas lamps, which just about lit up the area directly below them. When I was little, I used to think that the object of the gas lamp was to show you that there was a gas lamp. That's how poor the lighting was. They looked like stripped down scarecrows with arms outstretched. The reason for the arms was that every now and again a bloke with a big box-shaped barrow, containing brushes and a miniature v-shaped ladder, would come round to clean them. He'd prop his ladder up against the arm of the gas lamp, climb up and wash the windows with a brush and water.

Other tradesmen travelling the streets in the forties including glaziers, who'd travel round on a bike with a frame on each side, stacked with panes of glass in different sizes. The glazier would ride the streets looking for houses with cracked or broken windows. Martin Street was a particularly good hunting ground, what with the football and the other skirmishes that went on.

There was also a bloke who used to ride round once a week shouting, 'Oat cakes, pikelets.' Women and kids would rush out to buy them. He'd sell them from the basket on the front of his bike. These oat cakes and pikelets, after being warmed in the oven, were smothered in butter and were a very tasty addition to a sometimes regimented diet.

A bloke who sharpened scissors was another visitor to Martin Street. His bike would be transformed with a grindstone wheel and, once the bike was jacked up, he'd sharpen the knives and such by pedal power.

Another diversion that illustrates the naivety of the times, was when a gang of half a dozen kids once dashed past us on Martin Street, 'Where ya gooin'?' one of us shouted. Someone shouted back, 'Meda Street. Tha wants tu see it.' Straightaway, we joined the dash. By the time we got to Meadow Street, there must have been thirty or more kids. The venue? The butchers. The attraction? A new electric bacon slicer.

Sometimes, Dennis and I would go knocking on doors asking, 'Have you got any old papers?' Then, after we both had a bundle, we'd take them to the chip shop to be exchanged for a bag of chips apiece. We'd always ask, 'Can you put us some scrapings on, please?' These were the little droplets of fried batter that the chip shops routinely threw away but, when added to chips, were delicious. They still are.

Sometimes, when we had nothing to do we would go to the end of Martin Lane to watch the cobbler at work mending shoes in his little corner shop. This tiny little man sometimes seemed to be almost buried in shoes, bridles, horses' collars and all sorts of leatherwear. He was a nice little bloke with a hump on his back and didn't mind the intrusion of two or three small kids questioning him on what he was doing. He'd often give us a toffee apiece and chat away to us while working on his shoes. If any kid remarked that one of his shoes had a defect, he would often say, 'Let's have a look' and mend it free of charge. So, we'd have a chat, a sweet and our shoes mended for nowt.

Talking about the cobbler, brings to mind that, in the forties, there seemed to be more people around with humps on their backs than you see nowadays and, indeed, more people with visible disabilities, such as club feet, bow legs, permanent limps and people who walked in an exaggerated crippled way. There also seemed to be more kids who stuttered. Those days, if you cut yourself, within a day or so a yellow festering mark would circle the cut, probably due to a vitamin deficiency. As well as the obvious poor housing, shortage of food and general hardness of the times, the health of the people left a lot to be desired. It was a time when things like TB and diphtheria were rampant and, indeed, killers.

Money - or lack of it - seemed to be the root cause of misery and real suffering. I saw a graphic illustration of this when we were all at home one morning. For once, my dad was there when one of the neighbours popped their head in and shouted, 'Bailiffs are at bottom ot street.' My dad jumped up, telling us all to follow. I was thrilled to bits with excitement. When we got to the house at the bottom of the street, there was a wall of people standing on the pavement as a barricade against the bailiffs. The bailiffs' intention was to throw out a woman and her four kids from their house onto the street. Her husband had left her and she owed money. If they'd been successful, as well as rendering her homeless, the bailiffs would have commandeered anything in the house to compensate for what she owed. The noise that this wall of people made was almost deafening. All sorts of abuse was shouted at the bailiffs, who must have had some nerve because, for a while, they stood emotionless and stony-faced in their city three-piece suits, their 'I'm better than you' uniform. The local bobby accompanied them. Initially, we kids thought it was smashing, being encouraged to be little chuffs. And we didn't need much encouragement.

My dad, not one to mince words, targeted the local bobby, saying, 'Thar can fuck off for starters. We've just fought a fuckin' war. What for? For these twats to come waving their bits of paper?' The local bobby, clearly embarrassed by the situation, said, 'Ah don't want to be here, Fred.' To which the crowd began to bay and shout, 'Piss off then.'

The papers were pulled out of the bailiffs' hand and ripped up. Some bloke or other stepped out of the crowd to ask, 'Ow much does she owe, any rooad?' One of the bailiffs announced something like, 'Two pounds, seventeen and nine pence,' which only made matters worse. It was such a relatively small sum for such extreme treatment. Up to now, all us kids were loving every minute, but then things turned nastier. Someone shouted, 'Two fuckin' quid! A woman out ont streets for two fuckin, quid!' Someone grabbed one of the bailiffs - the other was already off down Martin Street like McDonald Bailey. There were shouts of 'String 'im up tut gas lamp. Hitler ought to 'ave wun t'war', and all sorts of things. The second bailiff struggled free and was off to follow his mate, with an astonishing tirade of abuse sending him on his way.

The bobby called for everyone to be calm and, after heated exchanges, things quietened down. All the neighbours then agreed to have a whip round to pay off the woman's debt, and agreed with the bobby that before he brought bailiffs onto Martin Street again, he'd consult with other residents first. That was the last time we saw bailiffs on Martin Street. The common sense of the bobby, allied to the good people of Martin Street, brought about the desired result of the woman and her kids keeping a roof over their heads and retaining what measly possessions they had.

The woman in question was comforted by the other women with, 'Come on luv, let's have a nice cup of tea,' which was said so often that I wondered what magical powers tea had because the saying followed all sorts of things, from someone giving birth, or someone dying, to someone suffering a multitude of injuries - even the end of the war. And I bet when war was declared it would have been followed by, 'I know, put kettle on, we'll have a cup of tea.' So

143

Mr Rington, whoever he was, should have been knighted for his services to humanity.

On a more serious note, the terrible plight of the woman could easily have been that of any one of the people involved in the fracas. Their reaction was a tremendous example of togetherness, the same attribute that helped everyone survive terrible times. As the song says, 'I'll get by with a little help from my friends.'

Chapter 20

Cats and dogs

The very successful post-a-cat caper was never repeated. It caused all sorts of consternation and theories on exactly how around twenty cats had managed to get into somebody's cellar. Underground tunnels was one, old Roman sewerage systems another. It came to an end because weeks after the cat job, my mother got wind of it. It came about when we went to the shops together. Fletchers on the corner of Martin Street was the nearest grocers. I'd been there, along with Pete and the others, to beg for cardboard boxes to use to transport the moggies to their destination, and avoid getting scratched. Anyway my mother and I walked in one day.

'Morning, Mrs Pass.'

'Morning, Luv, Ah'll have a quarter o' boiled 'am.'

'Right on, Luv. Ah see you've not flitted then?'

'Flitted?'

'Ay, flitted.'

'Who's telled ya wi flitted?'

'Your Fred 'ere (nodding down in my direction). He came in for sum cardboard boxes for cutlery.' (In fact, we had only four knives, four forks and four spoons. You'd have got them in your back pocket).

At this I started to blush, but tried to act as if I didn't know what was being said and started to peer out of the glass door. The grocer went on,

'I thought you'd come up in't world - all them boxes for cutlery.'
'Ay, well, wi changed us mind.'
'Will there be owt else, Luv?'
'No thanks.'

As soon as we got outside the inquisition started.

'What's tha been up to?'
'Nowt.'
'Ah bet it's summat to do wi them cats dahn't cellar an Ah 'no' nowt.'
'Cats?' (I say it as though she's talking about the Duckbilled Platypus or something).
'Ay, cats … chuffin' cats. Thi all owa t'place. Tha 'no's wor a cat is, dunt tha?'
'Oh, ya mean **cats**.' (I said it as though it had just come to me.)
'Ah'll bet owt that it were you and ya pals, ya little cowbag, who were shoving cats dahn't cellar grates.'

She'd got me banged to rights and, not knowing what to say next, I made a tragic mistake. She was getting extremely suspicious and what I then said proved to her beyond any doubt that I was involved in 'operation post-a-cat'.

'Yar 'air looks nice, mam.'

She blew her top (she'd never been to a hairdresser's in her life) and the conversation became one-way, not two.

'Ah've really had a belly full o' thee. I ought to have known. Chuffin' cats, chuffin' cats. Tha can keep away from Aistrop for a start, an' bleedin' Peter Marshall, 'n' Ah bet Jenkinson's got sommat to do wi it. Tha'll be for it, if 'e gets to 'no' about this lot, mi lad …'

She was going on and on, but I had turned down the volume of my hearing to such an extent that all I heard was a muffled grumbling. I had other things on my mind. I wondered if Dennis fancied a game of football, for a start.

Actually, though, I wonder if that escapade became the basis of a phobia about cats that I still have today. Not cats, exactly, but water. Whenever a cat had kittens, in those days, they'd be kept for a few days and then, if no one wanted them, they'd be drowned. I suppose it was an economic necessity. The drowning of the kittens was a sort of ritual performed by the women. (I've said before that the men went to work, and the women did almost everything else) A dustbin would have its contents emptied on the floor of the yard and then filled with water. The kittens would be held, one by one, under the water until they drowned. What was once a cute fluffy thing ended up like a wet dishcloth and chucked among the discarded ashes.

All the time this was happening, the mother cat would circle the bin in obvious apprehension and occasionally rear up on the bin on its hind legs. Kids stood round in morbid fascination and the stony silence would sometimes be interrupted by a nervous giggle. I always stood motionless, it was a sight I could have done without seeing. Little Pete always got the most upset (visually anyway) he'd rush around on Martin Street asking people if they wanted a kitten. When the drowning of the kittens had been completed they were shovelled up along with the discarded ashes back into the bin.

Around the time this once happened, my cousin Kenny called at our house. Kenny was my dad's sister Martha's lad and about five years older than me. Kenny was like a younger version of Uncle Ern, always 'up to something', as they say. I once spent a week with Aunt Martha, who was a lovely warm-hearted person, at their house on the Parson Cross council estate. Kenny kept pigeons, so we'd both be up at the crack of dawn. It was adventure just to be with Kenny. On one occasion, we were walking down a road on the 'Cross', when Kenny spotted a motorbike parked by a house. Straight away he said, 'Come on, we'll go for a ride', got the bike started and off we went across fields and all over the place in a sort of 'Steve McQueen' fashion. We had the motorbike all day, Kenny then returned it and no one was ever the wiser.

Well, when Kenny called at our house on this particular day, on his way out, he announced he was going to Glossop Road Baths and asked if I wanted to come, with a promise that he would teach

148

me how to swim. So, with my mother's approval, off we went to the baths. When we got changed, Kenny introduced me to the Baths by walking me along the side saying, 'This is the shallow end - and this is the deep end, and Ah'm going to show you how to swim.' He promptly got hold of an arm and a leg and threw me in the deep end. I was panic-stricken, floundering and swallowing water and thrashing about, and, after seeing the kittens, I could picture myself as a wet discarded dishcloth.

Kenny eventually pulled me out of the water, and couldn't stop laughing, saying, as I spluttered and gasped for breath, 'Ave a breather an' Ah'll chuck thi in agee'rn in a bit.' When Kenny dived in to have a swim while I got my breath back, I dashed off and got changed and ran home before he repeated the swimming lesson. Well, I can't swim to this day and if ever, on film or on television, there is a shot of water that's coming up to eye level, I feel a certain panic.

I also have a phobia about dogs, which can also probably be traced back to my formative years on Martin Street. Whenever there was a suitable number of men-folk working nights, a group of women would organise a sort of illicit card school. These card schools were always held at Mrs Stevenson's, who lived about ten yards up the street from us. My mother always 'made one' of these card schools and I went with her. I don't know what age I was, but I was young enough to be sat on her knee. The card school began at ten o'clock, usually on a Friday night, which meant that the players had a few pennies to play with. Mrs Stevenson was a sort of spindly, frizzy haired sort of women who smiled a lot. She had a wire-haired terrier of sorts, which seemed to be the reflection of herself. This dog never barked but always appeared to be watching me out of the corner of its eye. When the card game got underway, there I'd be, sitting on my mother's knee, with my legs dangling under the table. The dog (whose name escapes me) used to creep under the table and nip my legs and make me jump. It never drew blood by its nips so, when I complained, no one would believe me. Mrs Stevenson used to say, 'Never! He's as good as gold.' But such was the dog's stealth that I was always filled with apprehension.

These card games went on for quite a few years so that, by the time I was about eight years old, I had developed from spectator to dealer and, for my dealing, I would receive a few pennies from whoever won most that night. The games mostly played were Pontoon and Newmarket. Despite progressing to be a dealer of cards, Mrs Stevenson's little dog never failed to give me a nip.

The main culprit for my aversion to dogs, though, was Big Black Bruce. Bruce lived across the road from us on Martin Street, facing Mrs Stevenson's. The houses across had a small garden at the front and were considered, and indeed were, far superior to our old back-to-back. Big Bruce was a black mongrel dog who used to sit on the pavement in front of the passageway that led to its owner's house. It never bothered anyone but me. Pete, Dennis and Lawrence used to walk past opposite on their way to and from school. No trouble. But if I was with them, it would bark and snarl and chase me. It never caught me and never bit me - just sort of scared me off. It did a good job. Dennis and the gang were amused at this and would shout, 'Come on, Passey, it'll not hurt thee.' But as soon as I got opposite, it would go mad, chasing after me, barking. To emphasise how harmless this dog was towards the others, one Christmas time, Lawrence and Dennis trimmed up Bruce. They put a miniature bowler hat on his head, held on by a rubber band under his chin, some tinsel round his neck and even some plastic earrings clipped to his ears. My mother, for once, didn't have to ask if I'd had anything to do with it.

There was an occasion when another dog - a complete stranger - got the better of me. Pie and peas were a bit of a delicacy in those days and it was something of a treat when I was sent to the Hollow, pronounced 'hollah', in Albion Street just up the road from Martin Street. I'd take a basin and the woman there would put pies and peas and tasty gravy in. The only problem was coming back carrying the full, red-hot basin. I often had to stop to give my hands a cooling-off period, while I rested the pie and peas on somebody's brick wall. Once, while doing this and rubbing my burning hands together, I turned round in shock to see a pup nibbling away at the corner of one of the pies that was sticking up out of the gravy. I yelped at the shock of it. The pup yelped back and ran off. The pie was a bit of a mess so I pushed it under the peas in the gravy with my thumb. On getting back home, while she was dishing out the pie and peas, I heard my mother say, 'It looks like this pie's been half eaten.' It had. 'What's she think she's doin' geein' ya a pie like that?' I shrugged my shoulders. 'Ah've a good mind to send ya back'. She thought for a while. 'Oh, it dunt matter, I'll have it.' Well, it was her choice, I thought.

Chapter 21

Football, PE and the real world

Football played a big part in my life when I was young. Professional footballers in those days were just working class lads like the vast majority of their supporters. The only difference was that they had the talent to play the game we all loved, but get paid for it.

After about a dozen games or so in the 1951/52 season, Sheffield Wednesday introduced Derek Dooley. Derek soon started smashing in goals from all angles. He was instantly my hero. A Sheffield lad, Derek stood at six feet two and a half inches tall, had ginger hair and great big size twelve boots. He was a long-striding, fast-running centre forward. When in full flow, he was unstoppable, just like a runaway train. Autograph hunting was a hobby of mine and I would stand at the players' entrance before and after every game, collecting autographs. At one point, I had Derek's on every page and I never tired of asking him for his signature.

Once I wagged off school for the day to watch him train. There he was, on his own, in the heavy rain at Owlerton dog stadium being put through his paces by trainer Derek Brown who barked orders at him for about an hour. It was an amazing thing to watch. Brown never let up. 'Harder! Quicker!' he barked as Derek practiced his goal-scoring tactics, kicking a water-logged leather ball that looked like it weighed a ton, and running forward and backwards, non-stop. When the session was over, Derek trooped off the track, completely exhausted, looking like a horse who'd just completed the Grand National. Steam was coming off him all over and his shorts and shirt were stuck to him.

Not long ago, I read a biography of an old footballer who, while admitting that Dooley was a handful, said he was a lucky goal-scorer. I would counter that by saying the harder you train, the luckier you get.

As in all aspects of life for a kid in the '40s, improvisation was a key word when it came to playing football. I laughed at the absurdity of the story that a certain current footballer had a liking for wearing his wife's knickers. Well, in the '40s, I've seen kids playing in their mothers' knickers as part of their football kit. The elastic taken out of the legs and then dyed a suitable dark blue or black, they'd look just like the real McCoy. You'd also see lads stuff old Kit Carson comics down their football socks as improvised shin pads.

Football was 'the Game' for us and footballers were our idols. Once, when I was about eight years old, local youth clubs were given a game at which they were allowed to go around the ground with collection tins to raise money for needy youth clubs. The allocated game was Sheffield United versus Newcastle United at Bramall Lane. I was asked if I'd be one of the collectors. The prospect of going to Bramall Lane didn't appeal to me for obvious reasons, however, after being told that all collectors would enter the ground at the players' entrance, the game suddenly took on an overwhelming attraction. I thought I'd go in the players' entrance and, at the end of the match, I'd come out the same way giving me instant access to the players so that I could get their autographs. (Naturally, it was the Newcastle team which interested me. No self-respecting Wednesdayite would be seen dead asking a United player for his autograph.)

Well, I went along and did my collecting and, despite getting soaked though, the day was going smashing. United were getting soundly beaten and there was the prospect of those autographs looming. It could hardly have been better. I couldn't wait for the final whistle.

When the game was over, I approached this bloke with an armband on, which signified he was an official of the Youth Clubs' Association, to give him my tin. He pointed across the cricket pitch which joined the football pitch at the time and said that all collection tins had to be handed in at the cricket pavilion, so off I dashed.

I got there, only to find myself at the back of a queue of about thirty kids. It seemed to take an age and, all the time, I was worrying about getting the Newcastle players' autographs. As soon as my tin had been cashed in (a total of sixteen and ninepence), I was off, dashing towards the visitors' dressing room.

The door of the dressing room was ajar and, as I walked in, I was hit by an overwhelming smell of sweat and liniment and the view of scattered bits of turf and bandages strewed all over the floor. But, horror of horrors, there was nobody there. I felt free to curse out aloud. 'Oh, fuckin' 'ell.' From behind the half open door a voice boomed out, 'Stop that swearing, little fella.' I spun round and looked up. It was none other than the footballing legend Jackie Milburn, Newcastle's England international centre forward.

'What ya doin' in 'ere?' I've come fo' t'autographs,' I stuttered, not believing I was in the same room as this super-hero. 'Well, let's have a look, then,' said Jackie, indicating to my autograph book. I gave it to him. 'Way, laddie, you've got none.' 'No,' I said, 'I've been collecting fot youth clubs.' 'Well, give us ya pen then.' And he autographed my book.

But that wasn't the end of it. 'Come with me,' he said, and led me out to the Newcastle coach where all the other players were sat waiting for Jackie. He shouted to them. 'Quiet, lads, we've got a visitor.'

Then Jackie said to me, 'You tell me their names and I'll get them to sign your book.' So, down the coach we went. Jackie would point and say 'Who's this?' I'd say their name and Jackie would give them my book to sign. Joe Harvey, Frank Brennan, Bobby Mitchell, George Robeldo, Ernie Taylor and on and on. I was in total dreamland. Then all of a sudden Jackie stopped. 'Who's this?'

I stood staring and staring at this smiling bloke but I just couldn't recognise him. The coach was deadly silent as Jackie said, 'Well, what's his name?' 'Ah dunt 'no'', I muttered dejectedly. 'I didn't think you would cos 'e's our coach driver.' 'Thaz bin 'avin' me on', I said, as all the Newcastle players, along with Jackie, burst out laughing. Jackie then told me to say my goodbyes, which I did, while they all shouted theirs back to me.

I got off the coach, the proud possessor of all the Newcastle team's autographs and, as the coach pulled away, I waved and all the Newcastle players waived back. Jackie probably didn't realise it, but he made a 'soaked-as-a-rat' little kid's day with his attitude and spontaneous act of kindness. This incident happened over fifty years ago but the memory lingers on. When Jackie died in the 90s, thousands lined the street of Newcastle to pay homage. And you could add me to those thousands. He died leaving the legacy of the belief that money can't buy the respect of the working classes. Wor Jackie.

Football, whether watching the professionals or playing it in the street, was a marvellous escape into a fantasy world of dreams and heroes, as well as a way to learn about a game we all loved and admired. Our experience of sport in school, however, was a different ball game.

PE at Crookesmoor School usually meant two coconut mats placed in the playground and one of the pupils, usually a fat lad, bending down holding his ankles, pretending to be a box. We'd all line up and leapfrog over this unfortunate lad. I say unfortunate because it became a game, unbeknown to the teacher, to try and kick him up the arse deliberately accidentally, if you know what I mean. It was never a lesson I looked forward to because, if you fell on your face on the mat, it was like falling on barbed wire. And it was oh so repetitive that it was really boring when all I wanted to do was play football.

One particular hot and sunny day, our teacher announced that everyone should take off their shirts and trousers and that we would do our PE in our vests and pants. Dennis and I immediately protested but our objections were brushed aside by the teacher who refused to listen and told us all to form a line.

The problem for Dennis and me was that we didn't wear

underpants so we knew, when the line of forty-four boys was being formed, that the teacher was in for a shock. We all had to enter the yard from an entrance while the teacher stood by the fat kid waiting to watch us leapfrog over him.

I was the first in the line. The teacher, out of sight, gave his order. 'Right, start now!' I hurtled through the entrance wearing only my vest and shoes. And I was lucky to be wearing a vest. That had belonged to my older brother, Brian. The vest came to just below the knees but, as I leap-frogged over our human box, it became apparent that I wasn't wearing underwear. 'Oh, my God,' the teacher blurted, 'Stand over there!' Dennis was next. What made it worse for Dennis was that his vest was a sort of 'just under the rib cage' number and, when he ran, all his wiggly bits were really wiggling. 'STOP!!' the teacher shouted.

Everyone in our class was helpless by this time. The teacher suspended the lesson and went off, coming back soon after with two pairs of faded shorts, which he ordered Dennis and me to put on. 'Start again,' he bawled.

With my vest being so big, I'd got about a yard of vest protruding down each leg of my shorts. I must have looked like some sort of Christmas fairy. Dennis was next and he looked like something from another world. Everyone was still falling about, laughing. We completed our jumps and got back in line with the other forty-odd to repeat the exercise.

'I feel reight daft,' said Dennis. 'Ah, do. Ah'm gooin' 'ooerm', I replied. The others standing round us who heard said, 'Ah bet tha dern't.' That was enough for us. The back of the line was right up to the school gates, so I was out of sight of the teacher as I slipped through the gates. I was off to my mam on Martin Street.

As I walked down our entry I saw my mother donkey-stoning our step. The sight of me gave her a shock.

'What ya doin' back from school. And where's yor trousers and ya snake belt?'

'Ah got fed up.'

'Tha'll get fed up if tha's lost that snake belt, mi lad. It cost me one and six and Ah only bought it a month ago.' (Snake belts were supposed, ideally, to last from birth to starting work.)

'They're at school.'

'An' that's where yor goin' mi lad.'

She then grabbed me by the hand and took me back to school, all the way going on about the snake belt. By the time we arrived, the class had returned to the classroom. My mother then set about the teacher who, on spotting us, had greeted me with an, 'Oh, there you are, Freddy.'

'There you are, Freddy!? Where's his snake belt and trousers and what kind of a teacher are you to let kids go running out of school?'

'I'm sorry, Mrs Pass, but I have forty-four children to look after and it does have its difficult moments.'

'Difficult moments! Tha dun't 'no' what a difficult moment iz. You remember this. We all voted Labour and it's about time tha realised what's happening in the real world!'

Chapter 22

My Mother

My mother Gladys was born 3 March 1912 on Whitehouse Lane in the Upperthorpe district of Sheffield. Her parents were James and Mary Stones, my grandmother's name was Wragg. She was one of seven children, five girls and two boys. The girls were Alice, Annie, May, Elsie and the boys were Jim and Tom.

I suppose life, in many ways in the '40s, was more difficult for women than men, for while the men went to work to provide money, which, in those times was hardly enough to live on, in many cases the women stayed at home and bore the brunt of the day-to-day struggles. If I ever wanted anything, I'd try to avoid asking my dad. With any problems I had, I'd always go to my mother who used to say, 'Don't go bothering your dad,' or 'Don't tell your dad'. My dad would never miss work. It was his one source of pride, at a time when it was not unusual to see blokes with flat caps and white sweat towels going to work almost in droves. My mother would see us off to school, do housework, prepare meals and juggle finances on a daily basis. I've seen my mother spend a couple of hours filling the bath in front of the fire for when my dad got home from work and I've seen her peel off his sweat-soaked shirt because it was too wet for him to get off his own back. I suppose most of the tasks performed by mothers were thankless, hardly made better by mischievous kids like me.

One school parents' day stands out in my memory. Your

parents, or in my case, my mother, visited school while you were working and had a chat with the teacher about your progress. My dad would never attend such functions. I think he must have felt out of his depth talking to school teachers. The teacher in question wrote every child's surname on the blackboard and each child, in turn, had to fill in the first names of their parents. Then, after the visit, the child rubbed out the names of his or her parents. I remember one lad wrote 'Nellie' in front of his surname and, at playtime, everyone started calling him Nellie. So when the teacher said to me, 'Come along, Pass, write your parent's Christian name on the board,' following rapid consideration of more glamorous options, I wrote Joan, after the actress Joan Crawford. When I sat back down at my desk, I looked at the board and thought Joan Pass had a much better ring to it than Gladys.

The only problem with this was that, when my mother entered the classroom, the teacher asked, 'Mrs Pass?' to which my mother replied, 'Yes', but from then on the teacher kept referring to her as Joan. 'Well, Joan,' he started, 'your Fred's doing quite well,' and so the discussion went on. My mother kept giving me quizzical glances but never let on. Good owd mam.

Incidentally, I must mention that, during these visits, the teacher always had a personality change, he looked almost human, smiling even, and there was no sign of his stick. He was probably thinking something like 'I'll hit 'em all twice tomorrow.'

The thing about mothers then was that, if you ran in the house at any time of day with whatever problem, they were there, always the one you could run to. In my recollections of her, my mother always looked worried, which she probably was. I suppose the highlight of her week was payday and then she, not my dad, would take me to the Oxford cinema, and Saturday night when she would go to the Burlington pub with my dad.

In those days, when you took your marriage vow 'for better or worse', it would have been more accurate not to include the first part in most cases. The same goes for the 'richer or poorer' option. It was also obvious that women were second-class citizens. We once had a street trip to the seaside and my dad paid a couple of bob for my mother and me to go on it. He didn't go, but I remember my mother's face lighting up because we were going.

When my dad rejected a better paid job for reasons explained elsewhere, it was my mother who stood by him saying something like, 'We'll manage,' when it would have been easier to have insisted he stuck it out. Looking back on her life as a younger woman, it's hard to see what pleasure she got out of life at the time. She would have a tanner on the horses and, if she won - which was rare - she'd spend it on us. If she lost, it was, 'Don't tell yer dad.' Her favourite saying was that, 'There's always somebody worse off.' She said it right to her death at the age of eighty-odd, by then suffering with bad eyes, deaf, crippled with arthritis and goodness knows what else. She was still there to offer help and support to me to the day she died, in an old people's home. A mother to the last. It's just a pity that her closing days didn't have a few more laughs and contentment, but I can't pay her a bigger compliment than to say that she was and always will be my Mam.

Epilogue

Where are they now?

Peter Marshall

On leaving Martin Street, the Marshalls went to live on Wadsley Lane. We'd moved to Neepsend, Boyland Place. Pete found the moving a bit harder than we did and apparently missed his pals from Martin Street, so he became a regular visitor to our new house.

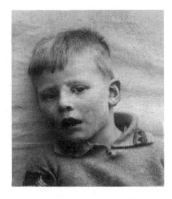

The last time he visited us was on 16 January 1954. If you wonder how I've managed to remember the date and year of his visit, it is because he died the next day Sunday, 17 January 1954. He came on the Saturday and we played football in our back yard. On this particular day we fell out, ironically the only time we ever fell out. We were playing football and an unwritten rule was that, if you kicked the ball over the wall, you fetched it. Well in this particular game, I kicked the ball, it hit Pete's shoulder and bounced over the wall. I, wrongly, said he should fetch it to which he replied, 'No chance,' so we fell out. He ran off and we both shouted names at each other. I thought no more about it, thinking he'd be back next week and we'd be pals again.

The following evening Mr and Mrs Marshall visited our house. They said they'd come from the Infirmary Hospital and that they'd lost Pete. I thought, when they said they'd lost him, they meant they couldn't find him. I didn't know it was a euphemism for death. Oh, I couldn't believe it. Little Pete had died aged eleven years old. Apparently he'd complained of headaches and when they put him to bed, he began screaming with pain. The Marshalls sent for an ambulance but, within minutes of him arriving at the Infirmary, he was pronounced dead. Poor Pete always looked a forlorn little figure and he was now gone forever, and we'd parted on bad terms after all the laughs we'd had and all the pranks we'd got up to.

His funeral was the following Saturday morning, 23 January, at Burngreave Cemetery. It was a perfect day for two reasons. The first was that the skies were black, and it thundered and rained cats and dogs. As they lowered his little coffin down in the grave, there was a loud clap of thunder and, just when it seemed it couldn't rain any harder, it did. The weather seemed really appropriate for such a terrible loss and a terrible occasion.

His mother had just given birth to a little girl, ironically on 17 December. I'm sure having a newborn helped Mrs Marshall overcome her loss.

The other thing that made the day perfect was the fact that Wednesday were playing United at Hillsborough and Pete and I were Wednesday-ites and had planned for weeks to go to the match together. Well, I went on my own and thought to myself that Wednesday had to win for Pete - and they did, three-two. Pete would have liked that.

The only consolation about losing a pal at such a young age is that, in your memory, as in Pete's case, they're always remembered as a little kid. I can still picture him now. Sandy hair, freckled face, hob nail boots, one sock up, the other sock down, and his long-short trousers. Pete always wore a smile, except when he was performing his crying act. Well, Pete, there was a lot of crying in Burngreave Cemetery on January 23 and no one was acting.

Lawrence Jenkinson

Lawrence had ginger hair and a most unusual feature. He had wobbly eyes, which you could refer to, if you wanted to be cruel - and out of punching distance. Lawrence passed his eleven-plus and went on to grammar school. In our group, Lawrence was the one with the orderly mind, he also had a little daring about him, which is reflected in his success in business.

Of the three of us who are left, Lawrence has been, by far, the most successful. His is 'Lawrence Jenkinson's Opticians' and is extremely successful, reflected in the fact that he owns several optical dispensaries across Sheffield. Both his mam and dad worked full-time, mainly for Jenks' benefit. He always seemed better turned out than the rest of us, and in comparison to our house, their house seemed much warmer and cosier than ours. But despite what he has today, Jenks knows the hard edge of life, of that there is no doubt. For me, it's good to see him do so well for himself. It's one-up for Martin Street and I hope he goes on, if he wants, to own fifty opticians' shops. Jenks lives in the Bradway area and has three children - two boys and a girl. His mother is still alive. She was always kind to me as a little kid, which I probably made hard for people at times.

Dennis Aistrop

Dennis was the brains of the outfit, no doubt about that, and while he didn't go on to gain the academic qualifications he could have done, he's now in a good position, where he doesn't have to work. Good luck to him. He still owes his mother a lot for the fact that he survived the terrible conditions and hard times of the Martin Street days.

Lawrence had one over Dennis in that he was the only child of parents who, by both working, ensured that he would have a secure future one way or another. Dennis passed his eleven-plus, too, but whereas Dennis's family couldn't afford the money for the uniform and the rest of the kit, Lawrence's parents could.

Fred Pass

As for me, I married Sandra and we have three children - Mark, Jonathan and Jill and, to date, three grandchildren, Harry James FitzPatrick, Frankie Joseph Fitzpatrick and Lydia Mia Pass. I spent forty years working in scrap yards and there are no Bamber Gasgoines in scrap yards. I've never met one anyway. And something's just dawned on me, I'm spending my time writing about how well everyone else has done. Sad init?

Imagination was my strong point, so I'm left imagining what

I'd do if I had the other two's money (joke). We were a happy lot during hard times. I've never forgotten them and I know I never will.